COMPREHENSIVE RESEARCH
AND STUDY GUIDE

Thomas Hardy

BLOOM'S
MAJOR
POETS

EDITED AND WITH AN INTRODUCTION
BY HAROLD BLOOM

CURRENTLY AVAILABLE

COMPREHENSIVE RESEARCH
AND STUDY GUIDE

Thomas Hardy

CHELSEA HOUSE
PUBLISHERS
A Haights Cross Communications Company
Philadelphia

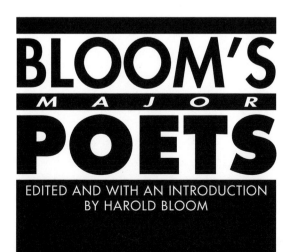

BLOOM'S MAJOR POETS

EDITED AND WITH AN INTRODUCTION
BY HAROLD BLOOM

Printed and bound in the United States of America.

First Printing
1 3 5 7 9 8 6 4 2

Library of Congress Cataloging-in-Publication Data

Thomas Hardy / [edited by] Harold Bloom.
    p. cm. — (Bloom's major poets)
  Includes index.
  ISBN 0-7910-7891-4
  1. Hardy, Thomas, 1840-1928—Poetic works. I. Bloom, Harold. II.
Series.
  PR4757.P58T48 2004
  821'.8—dc22

                                                    2004003702

Contributing Editor: Janyce Marson
Cover design by Keith Trego
Layout by EJB Publishing Services

CONTENTS

USER'S GUIDE

This volume is designed to present biographical, critical, and bibliographical information on the author and the author's best-known or most important poems. Following Harold Bloom's editor's note and introduction is a concise biography of the author that discusses major life events and important literary accomplishments. A critical analysis of each poem follows, tracing significant themes, patterns, and motifs in the work. As with any study guide, it is recommended that the reader read the poem beforehand and have a copy of the poem being discussed available for quick reference.

A selection of critical extracts, derived from previously published material, follows each thematic analysis. In most cases, these extracts represent the best analysis available from a number of leading critics. Because these extracts are derived from previously published material, they will include the original notations and references when available. Each extract is cited, and readers are encouraged to check the original publication as they continue their research. A bibliography of the author's writings, a list of additional books and articles on the author and their work, and an index of themes and ideas conclude the volume.

ABOUT THE EDITOR

Harold Bloom is Sterling Professor of the Humanities at Yale University. He is the author of over 20 books, and the editor of more than 30 anthologies of literary criticism.

Professor Bloom's works include *Shelley's Mythmaking* (1959), *The Visionary Company* (1961), *Blake's Apocalypse* (1963), *Yeats* (1970), *A Map of Misreading* (1975), *Kabbalah and Criticism* (1975), *Agon: Toward a Theory of Revisionism* (1982), *The American Religion* (1992), *The Western Canon* (1994), and *Omens of Millennium: The Gnosis of Angels, Dreams, and Resurrection* (1996). *The Anxiety of Influence* (1973) sets forth Professor Bloom's provocative theory of the literary relationships between the great writers and their predecessors. His most recent books include *Shakespeare: The Invention of the Human*, a 1998 National Book Award finalist, *How to Read and Why* (2000), *Stories and Poems for Extremely Intelligent Children of All Ages* (2001), *Genius: A Mosaic of One Hundred Exemplary Creative Minds* (2002), and *Hamlet: Poem Unlimited* (2003).

Professor Bloom earned his Ph.D. from Yale University in 1955 and has served on the Yale faculty since then. He is a 1985 MacArthur Foundation Award recipient and served as the Charles Eliot Norton Professor of Poetry at Harvard University in 1987–88. In 1999 he was awarded the prestigious American Academy of Arts and Letters Gold Medal for Criticism. Professor Bloom is the editor of several other Chelsea House series in literary criticism, including BLOOM'S MAJOR SHORT STORY WRITERS, BLOOM'S MAJOR NOVELISTS, BLOOM'S MAJOR DRAMATISTS, BLOOM'S MODERN CRITICAL INTERPRETATIONS, BLOOM'S MODERN CRITICAL VIEWS, BLOOM'S BIOCRITIQUES, BLOOM'S GUIDES, BLOOM'S MAJOR LITERARY CHARACTERS, and BLOOM'S PERIOD STUDIES.

EDITOR'S NOTE

My Introduction centers upon Thomas Hardy's last book of poems, *Winter Words*, and upon its exemplification of Shelley's lifelong influence upon Hardy.

As this little volume gives more than thirty critical extracts dealing with six of Hardy's strongest poems, I can indicate here only a few that are of particular interest to me. These include Robert Langbaum upon "Hap," Samuel Hynes on "Neutral Tones," and John Paul Riquelme on "During Wind and Rain."

"The Convergence of the Twain" is commended for its inventiveness by William H. Pritchard, while John Bayley and Barbara Hardy equally are eloquent upon "The Darkling Thrush." Hardy's personal history is related by Trevor Johnson to the elegiac "Afterwards."

Harold Bloom

Only a poet challenges a poet as poet, and so only a poet makes a poet. To the poet-in-a-poet, a poem is always *the other man*, the precursor, and so a poem is always a person, always the father of one's Second Birth. To live, the poet must *misinterpret* the father, by the crucial act of misprision, which is the re-writing of the father.

But who, what is the poetic father? The voice of the other, of the *daimon*, is always speaking in one; the voice that cannot die because already it has survived death—*the dead poet lives in one*. In the last phase of strong poets, they attempt to join the undying by living in the *dead poets* who are already alive in them. This late Return of the Dead recalls us, as readers, to a recognition of the original motive for the catastrophe of poetic incarnation. Vico, who identified the origins of poetry with the impulse towards divination (to foretell, but also to become a god by foretelling), implicitly understood (as did Emerson, and Wordsworth) that a poem is written to escape dying. Literally, poems are refusals of mortality. Every poem therefore has two makers: the precursor, and the ephebe's rejected mortality.

A poet, I argue in consequence, is not so much a man speaking to men as a man rebelling against being spoken to by a dead man (the precursor) outrageously more alive than himself. A poet dare not regard himself as being *late*, yet cannot accept a substitute for the first vision he reflectively judges to have been his precursor's also. Perhaps this is why the poet-in-a-poet *cannot marry*, whatever the person-in-a-poet chooses to have done.

Poetic influence, in the sense I give to it, has almost nothing to do with the verbal resemblances between one poet and another. Hardy, on the surface, scarcely resembles Shelley, his prime precursor, but then Browning, who resembles Shelley even less, was yet more fully Shelley's ephebe than even Hardy was. The same observation can be made of Swinburne and of Yeats in relation to Shelley. What Blake called the Spiritual Form, at once the aboriginal poetical self and the True Subject, is what the ephebe is so dangerously obliged to the precursor for even possessing. Poets need not *look* like their fathers, and the anxiety of influence more frequently than not is quite distinct from the anxiety of style. Since poetic influence is necessarily misprision, a taking or doing amiss of one's burden, it is to be expected that such a process of malformation and misinterpretation will, at the very least, produce deviations in style between strong poets. Let us remember always Emerson's insistence as to what it is that makes a poem:

> For it is not meters, but a meter-making argument that makes a poem,—a thought so passionate and alive that like the spirit of a plant or an animal it has an architecture of its own, and adorns nature with a new thing. The thought and the form are equal in the order of time, but in the order of genesis the thought is prior to the form. The poet has a new thought; he has a whole new experience to unfold; he will tell us how it was with him, and all men will be the richer in his fortune. For the experience of each new age requires a new confession, and the world seems always waiting for its poet....
>
> ("The Poet")

Emerson would not acknowledge that meter-making arguments themselves were subject to the tyrannies of inheritance, but that they are so subject is the saddest truth I know about poets and poetry. In Hardy's best poems, the central meter-making argument is what might be called a skeptical lament for the hopeless incongruity of ends and means in all human acts. Love and the means of love cannot be brought together, and the truest name for the human condition is simply that it is loss:

> And brightest things that are theirs....
>   Ah, no; the years, the years;
> Down their carved names the raindrop plows.

These are the closing lines of "During Wind and Rain," as good a poem as our century has given us. The poem, like so many others, is a grandchild of the "Ode to the West Wind," as much as Stevens' "The Course of a Particular" or any number of major lyrics by Yeats. A carrion-eater, Old Style, would challenge my observations, and to such a challenge I could offer, in its own terms, only the first appearance of the refrain:

Ah, no; the years O!
How the sick leaves reel down in throngs!

But such terms can be ignored. Poetic influence, between strong poets, works in the depths, as all love antithetically works. At the center of Hardy's verse, whether in the early *Wessex Poems* or the late *Winter Words*, is this vision:

And much I grieved to think how power and will
In opposition rule our mortal day,

And why God made irreconcilable
Good and the means of good; and for despair
I half disdained mine eyes' desire to fill

With the spent vision of the times that were
And scarce have ceased to be—

Shelley's *The Triumph of Life* can give us also the heroic motto for the major characters in Hardy's novels: "For in the battle Life and they did wage, / She remained conqueror." The motto would serve as well for the superb volume *Winter Words in Various Moods and Metres*, published on October 2 in 1928, the year that Hardy died on January 11. Hardy had hoped to publish the book on June 2, 1928, which would have been his eighty-eighth birthday. Though a few poems in the book go back as far as the 1860's, most were written after the appearance of Hardy's volume of lyrics, *Human Shows*, in 1925. A few books of twentieth-century verse in English compare with *Winter Words* in greatness, but very few. Though the collection is diverse, and has no central design, its emergent theme is a counterpoise to the burden of poetic incarnation, and might be called the Return of the Dead, who haunt Hardy as he faces towards death.

In his early poem (1887), *Shelley Skylark*, Hardy, writing rather in the style of his fellow Shelleyan, Browning, speaks of his ancestor's "ecstatic heights in thought and rhyme." Recent critics who admire Shelley are not particularly fond of "To a Skylark," and it is rather too ecstatic for most varieties of modern sensibility, but we can surmise why it so moved Hardy:

> We look before and after,
>   And pine for what is not:
> Our sincerest laughter
>   With some pain is fraught;
> Our sweetest songs are those that tell of saddest thought.
>
> Yet if we could scorn
>   Hate, and pride, and fear;
> If we were things born
>   Not to shed a tear,
> I know not how thy joy we ever should come near.

The thought here, as elsewhere in Shelley, is not so simple as it may seem. Our divided consciousness, keeping us from being able to unperplex joy from pain, and ruining the presentness of the moment, at least brings us an aesthetic gain. But even if we lacked our range of negative affections, even if grief were not our birthright, the pure joy of the lark's song would still surpass us. We may think of Shelleyan ladies like Marty South, and even more Sue Bridehead, who seems to have emerged from the *Epipsychidion*. Or perhaps we may remember Angel Clare, as a kind of parody of Shelley himself. Hardy's Shelley is very close to the most central of Shelleys, the visionary skeptic, whose head and whose heart could never be reconciled, for they both told truths, but contrary truths. In *Prometheus Unbound*, we are told that in our life the shadow cast by love is always ruin, which is the head's report, but the heart in Shelley goes on saying that if there is to be coherence at all, it must come through Eros.

Winter Words, as befits a man going into his later eighties, is more in ruin's shadow than in love's realm. The last poem, written in 1927, is called *He Resolves To Say No More*, and follows directly on "*We Are Getting to The End*," which may be the bleakest sonnet in the language. Both poems explicitly reject any vision of hope, and are set against the Shelleyan rational meliorism of *Prometheus Unbound*. "We are getting to the end of visioning / The impossible within this universe," Hardy flatly insists, and he recalls Shelley's vision of rolling time backward, only to dismiss it as the doctrine of Shelley's Ahasuerus: "(Magians who drive the midnight quill / With brain aglow / Can see it so)". Behind this rejection is the mystery of misprision, of deep poetic influence in its final phase, which I have called *Apophrades* or the Return of the Dead. Hovering everywhere in *Winter Words*, though far less explicitly than it hovers in *The Dynasts*, is Shelley *Hellas*. The peculiar strength and achievement of *Winter Words* is not that we are compelled to remember Shelley when we read in it, but rather that it makes us read much of Shelley as though Hardy were Shelley's ancestor, the dark father whom the revolutionary idealist failed to cast out.

Nearly every poem in *Winter Words* has a poignance unusual even in Hardy, but I am moved most by "He Never Expected Much," the poet's reflection on his eighty-sixth birthday, where his dialogue with the "World" attains a resolution:

"I do not promise overmuch,
    Child; overmuch;
Just neutral-tinted haps and such,"
    You said to minds like mine.
Wise warning for your credit's sake!
Which I for one failed not to take,
And hence could stem such strain and ache
    As each year might assign.

The "neutral-tinted haps," so supremely hard to get into poems, are the staple of Hardy's achievement in verse, and contrast both to Wordsworth's "sober coloring" and Shelley's "deep autumnal tone." All through *Winter Words* the attentive reader will hear a chastened return of High Romantic Idealism, but muted into Hardy's tonality. Where Yeats malformed both himself and his High Romantic fathers, Blake and Shelley, in the violences of *Last Poems and Plays*, Hardy more effectively subdued the questing temperaments of his fathers, Shelley and

Browning, in *Winter Words*. The wrestling with the great dead is subtler in Hardy, and kinder both to himself and to the fathers.

Hardy's Shelley was essentially the darker poet of *Adonais* and *The Triumph of Life*, though I find more quotations from *The Revolt of Islam* scattered through the novels than from any other single work by Shelley, and I suppose *Hellas* and *Prometheus Unbound* were even more direct, technical influences upon *The Dynasts*. But Hardy was one of those young men who went about in the 1860's carrying a volume of Shelley in his pocket. Quite simply, he identified Shelley's voice with poetry itself, and though he could allow his ironic sense to touch other writers, he kept Shelley inviolate, almost as a kind of secular Christ. His misprision of Shelley, his subversion of Shelley's influence, was an unconscious defense, quite unlike the overt struggle against Shelley of Browning and Yeats.

American poets, far more than British, have rebelled overtly against ancestral voices, partly because of Whitman's example, and also because of Emerson's polemic against the very idea of influence, his insistence that going alone must mean refusing even the good models, and so entails reading primarily as an inventor. Our greater emphasis upon originality has produced inversely a more malevolent anxiety of influence, and our poets consequently misinterpret their precursors more radically than do the British. Hardy's was a gentler case of influence-anxiety than that of any other modern strong poet, for reasons allied, I think, to the astonishing ease of Hardy's initial entrance into his poethood.

Thomas Hardy

Thomas Hardy was born on June 2, 1840, in Upper Bockhampton, an area of southwest England that he was to make the "Wessex" of his novels. At that time, Upper Bockhampton was relatively untouched by the social changes and industrialization which were transforming other parts of England. The vast railway system that had been spreading its network across the country in the 1820's and 1830's would not reach Dorset county until 1847. A small but important agricultural center for the surrounding region, Dorset maintained its folk traditions, and those traditions play a vital role in several of Hardy's novels. However, the encroaching forces of an increasingly mechanized world were challenging these traditions. It is against this background of agricultural labor and such ancient monuments as Stonehenge, that Hardy's characters and poems try to find reprieve. Indeed, they oftentimes seek to find hope and salvation by adhering to the time-tested rhythms of a pastoral labor and rural celebration. However, the men and women in Hardy's novels are not in complete control of their fate but, rather, subject to the mercy of indifferent forces that dictate their behavior and their relationship with others. Nevertheless, outside forces notwithstanding, fate is not a wholly external force and characters are driven by the demands of their own nature as much as by anything from outside them.

Both his father and grandfather, alike named Thomas Hardy, were stone-masons, although his father was not very ambitious. His mother, Jemima Hand, was an unusually well-read woman, fond of reciting ballads. Hardy described her as possessing a "wonderful vitality," but instilled with the ancient pessimism of the rural poor. Before he started school, young Thomas Hardy had learned to play the violin and was already fond of music and dance. Hardy's formal education lasted for about eight years in local schools, first, in 1848, at a school in the nearby village presided over by the childless Mrs. Julia Augusta Martin. It is around this time that Hardy's mother gave him Dryden's *Virgil*, Johnson's *Rasselas*, and Saint-Pierre's *Paul and Virginia*, and he found his grandfather's copy of the periodical *A History of the Wars*, which dealt with the Napoleonic wars. Michael Millgate says that it was at his first school that Hardy "suffered the earliest experiences of love [for Mrs. Martin], the slighting of the loved one, and the subsequent guilt which were to recur throughout his life" (*Thomas Hardy: A Biography*.) In 1849, Hardy was transferred to a school in Dorchester, primarily because the headmaster was an excellent teacher of Latin. Hardy became well-read in English, French and Latin, enjoying such works as James Grant's *The Scottish Cavalier* and Shakespeare's tragedies. It was also around this time, that Hardy also observed first-hand some of the peasant folkways such as the Christmas mummers, village dancing around a maypole, and the sight of a prisoner in the stocks at Puddletown. At Christmas in 1854, he was presented with a book entitled *Scenes & Advertures at Home and Abroad*, a prize he won for diligence and good behavior.

In 1856, Hardy left school and was apprenticed for the next three years to John Hicks, a Dorchester architect and church-restorer, for whom his father had worked. Hicks was a genial and well-educated man in his forties, from whom Hardy received instruction in "architectural drawing and surveying." During these days there was an enthusiastic demand for "medievalism" and religious revivalism, a type of restoration work with which Hicks was primarily engaged. Hardy would later write in "Memories of Church Restoration," that he most lamented the interruption of ancient traditions, a feeling that is evidenced throughout his literary works. He also believed that with his imperfect knowledge of Latin and scant knowledge of Greek he was ill-prepared for university admission. As a result of an acute awareness of these deficiencies, Hardy determined to embark on a rigorous program of self-education. He continued to study Latin and began learning Greek, with much of his reading taking place between five and eight in the morning. It was at this time that he enjoyed the privilege of meeting one of his neighbors, Mr. William Barnes, a Dorchester schoolmaster and dialect poet of distinction. Then on August 9, Hardy witnessed the execution of Martha Brown for the murder of her husband. It was to leave a lasting impression in his mind and no doubt contributed to the final scene in *Tess of the d'Urbervilles*.

From 1858 to 1861, Hardy began writing poems, among them "Domicilium," the earliest of his poems to be preserved. He was now assisted in Greek by Horace Moule, eight years his senior and the son of a prominent minister. Because of his inability to pass mathematics, Moule left both Oxford and Cambridge without a degree. Nevertheless, he managed to win the Hulsean Prize at Cambridge for his work on *Christian Oratory*. That work was published in 1859. He would remain a close friend of Hardy, offering advice and assistance in promoting his protégé's literary career. It has been acknowledged by scholars that Moule influenced Hardy's thinking on modern topics and that Hardy followed the *Saturday Review* for which Moule wrote, particularly on issues concerning the controversy between science and Christian orthodoxy. Moule's suicide in 1873 would have a profound effect on Hardy.

Throughout his life, Thomas Hardy would retain a wide-ranging intellectual curiosity in literary, philosophical, and theological issues. In the spring of 1863 he heard Dickens lecture and in September 1864 he went to the London School of Phrenology to have his head read by the proprietor. Like many others, Hardy would undergo a crisis of faith, precipitated by, among other things, his reading Darwin's *Origin of Species*, of which he counted himself as among the earliest readers, and the controversial theological symposium, *Essays and Reviews* (1860), the latter causing Hardy to abandon the Christianity of his childhood.

On April 17, 1862, his apprenticeship with Hicks now over, the twenty-one year old Thomas Hardy set out for London, which, at this time, was the center of an unprecedented urban growth. He immediately found employment there with Arthur Blomfield, who was in need of a "young Gothic draughtsman" to assist in the restoration and design of churches and rectory-houses. According to Millgate, "his attraction to the Church seems always to have depended not so much upon intellectual conviction as upon the emotion appeal of its rituals and, later, upon its perceived possibilities as an avenue of social and especially educational advancement." Nevertheless, as his literary work demonstrates, he retained a thorough knowledge of the Bible and an interest in church architecture.

From 1862 to 1867, Hardy treasured and sought to preserve the customs, manners, and ways of life that were quickly fading out. And during this period, he spent his leisure time reading a great deal of Shakespeare from a ten-volume edition he had just purchased, in addition to reading works which would provide a model for argumentative prose. Hardy also demonstrated a love of music, an interest he shared with Blomfield. He took up the violin while, at the same time, methodically reading the *Old Testament* and all of the major poets, including Spenser, Shakespeare, Burns, Byron, Wordsworth, Tennyson, William Barnes, and especially Swinburne, of whose *Poems and Ballads* (1866) Hardy was enamored. He also began writing poetry during the period of 1865–1867, which he submitted to the magazines. However, this first attempt at poetry writing was a failure, which resulted in his destroying many of the poems that he considered to be of the poorest quality. Nevertheless, as F.B. Pinion remarks, many of these poems "are remarkable in their relentless confrontation of the truth, however chilling. Love deceives; beauty is subject to the ravages of time; and chance and indifference rule the universe." (*A Hardy Companion*) These deeply felt convictions were borne of his readings in science where concepts of the universe and the individual's importance within this cosmic scheme were changing. Similarly, science was having a profound impact on Hardy's religious beliefs, such that the universe was now considered neutral and indifferent. In addition, Hardy had a great love for animals and his writings repeatedly demonstrate his concern for their suffering. Furthermore, the reality of the publishing industry was that fiction was a far more marketable and lucrative genre. His first novel, *The Poor Man and the Lady*, a social satire written in 1863, remained unpublished, having been rejected by the publishers in 1868 on the recommendation of George Meredith. Nevertheless, despite his criticism, Meredith advised Hardy to continue writing, the result of which advice was *Desperate*

Remedies, published anonymously in 1871. Published in the conventional and expensive three-volume form, it was similar to the very popular sensational novels of Wilkie Collins and others, but its reception was very unenthusiastic. The *Athenaeum* review of April 1871 described it as "an unpleasant story" while the *Spectator* review, also in April of 1871, called it "disagreeable, and not striking in any way," while lauding Hardy's skill in depicting rural life.

The following year saw Hardy's career as a novelist successfully launched with the publication of *Under the Greenwood Tree* in 1872; his shortest novel quickly became a classic. Hardy's friend, Horace Moule, an accomplished classical scholar and writer on the contemporary debate between science and Christian orthodoxy, praised the work. Moule described it as "the best prose idyll we have seen for a long while past." Interestingly, Moule's critique points out the influence of George Eliot's early work in addition to *Silas Marner*. Furthermore, Hardy's subtitle to this work, *A Rural Painting of the Dutch School*, is a phrase to be found in *Adam Bede* where realistic portraits of peasant life are being compared to seventeenth century Dutch art. Above all else, however, *Under the Greenwood Tree* is a love story that ends with the marriage of the heroine, Fancy Day, to the unassuming Dick Dewey. It is also a story in which social conditions are crucial, and about a world in which the old ways of the village are losing ground to mechanical interventions as the traditional church band is in the process of being replaced by the organ. And, as a result of his new success, Hardy would soon give up his architectural work and begin producing a series of novels that would end with *Jude the Obscure* in 1896, when the hostile reception of this novel sent him back to poetry.

In 1870, during his travel to St. Juliot on the coast of Cornwall on architectural business, Hardy began a long courtship with Emma Lavinia Gifford, the sister-in-law of the local clergyman. Emma Lavinia, who came from a middle class family and whose uncle was an archdeacon, was of a higher social status than Thomas Hardy. Despite opposition from both their families, the couple later married on September 17, 1874. Hardy's earning capacity had increased with the success of *Far From the Madding*

Crowd, which in turn enabled him to devote his energies full time to the writing profession. In fact, their wedding, which was held in London and at which no member of his own family was in attendance, took place while *Far From the Madding Crowd* was appearing in the *Cornhill*. Nevertheless, the marriage which began happily would later cause great heartache and bitterness. Although supportive of Hardy's literary career, Emma was obsessed with her social superiority and her own writing talents. She was also very much opposed to the subject matter of *Jude the Obscure* and even tried to prevent its publication.

During this busy and fruitful time of 1871, Hardy was also planning his next novel, *A Pair of Blue Eyes*, a story focused on social differences and their impact on love relationships, namely that of the heroine, Elfride Swancourt, who is loved by two men—Stephen Smith, "a rural builder's son" and Henry Knight, an urbane intellectual. Most significantly, however, is a scene that gives the reader a glimpse at the Victorian awareness of scientific discoveries and new concepts of space and time; here, the immensity of geological time with the corresponding diminution of human life. While Henry Knight is hanging from a cliff and about to fall to his death, he observes "an imbedded fossil.... It was one of the early crustaceans called Trilobites. Separated by millions of years in their lives, Knight and this underling seem to have met in their place of death." *A Pair of Blue Eyes* contains some important autobiographical features, including Henry Knight's resemblance to Horace Moule, a Dorchester friend and Cambridge man, who played an important part in the young Thomas Hardy's process of self-education. Moule's suicide in September, 1873 was a tremendous blow to Thomas Hardy. Robert Gittings marks Moule's death as Hardy's transformation into a "a fully tragic artist, an expounder of man's true miseries." Finally, the publishing history of *A Pair of Blue Eyes* is also important. Before it was published in its final volume form in 1873, it was first serialized in 1872. This serialization was to set a precedent whereby all of Hardy's subsequent novels would make their initial appearance as episodes in a periodical, in this instance, *Tinselys' Magazine*.

Hardy's success as a novelist continued to mount with the

publication of *The Hand of Ethelberta* in 1876, *The Return of the Native* in 1878, and a minor novel, *The Trumpet-Major*, in 1880. By this time, Hardy had established himself in a London suburb where he was near the literary circles of the day, dining out regularly, meeting celebrities, and taking occasional vacations on the Continent with his wife, although in 1880 they still had no permanent home. It was here that he also formed lasting friendships, among them the London writer and critic Edmund Gosse whom he had met at the Savile Club. However, 1880 also marked a setback when Hardy became seriously ill with an internal hemorrhage. He remained in bed for several months, all the while dictating his novel, *Laodicean*, to Emma. The least successful of his novels, its hero is an architect and the heroine an heiress, while the narrative is replete with the trappings of Victorian melodrama and intrigue. Upon his recovery in the spring of 1881, Hardy and his wife set out to find a house in Hardy's native county of Dorset, and in 1882 he published his third minor novel, *Two on a Tower*. Here, the hero is a young astronomer, Swithin St. Cleeve, romantically involved with a high-born woman, Lady Constantine, set amidst the background of "the stellar universe." After settling in Wimborne Minster in 1881, Hardy laid some roots in Dorset by joining such groups as the Dorset Natual History and Antiquarian Field Club. He also spent considerable time in London with literary personalities in clubs, salons and dinner parties. Nevertheless, Hardy's financial position was strong and he set to building a house according to his own design outside Dorchester. The house would be called Max Gate (after Henry Mack, a former toll-gate keeper of the neighborhood) and the couple took up residence in June 1885. Hardy would remain there for the rest of his life.

The move to Dorchester was to influence Hardy's creative life and influenced the first novel he wrote after returning to Dorchester, *The Mayor of Casterbridge*, which he began writing in 1884 and completed in April 1885. *The Mayor of Casterbridge*, which takes place around the mid-19th century, therefore going back a generation before the date of composition, is suffused with a profound sense of loss and the destruction of a way of life by fate, historical and social circumstances, and the misguided judgment of certain characters. Though professional reviewers did not appreciate the novel, George Gissing, Robert Louis Stevenson, and Gerard Manley Hopkins had praise for *The Mayor of Casterbridge.*

In November 1885, Hardy began *The Woodlanders* with a new burst of energy that characterized his return to his native Dorset. The novel was not well received by some Victorian reviewers who were disturbed by Hardy's insistence on taking up highly controversial moral and social issues. On the other hand, the *Athenaeum* found the novel to be "simply perfect." This was followed by, among other works, *Tess of the d'Urbervilles* in 1891 and an essay, "Candour in English Fiction," published in the *New Review* in January 1890. The "Candour" essay focuses on the "fearful price" that a principled artist pays for "the privilege of writing in the English language," due to the pressures exerted by editors and librarians and the existence of the "young person" standard. For Hardy, life is "a physiological fact" and "its honest portrayal must be largely concerned with, for one thing, the relations of the sexes." Following the controversy of *Jude the Obscure*, Hardy never wrote another novel. The story entitled *On the Western Circuit*, published the same year as *Tess*, similarly focused on a country girl seduced by a sophisticated city man, her "ruin" leads, ironically, to his ruin and a lifetime of misery for all concerned.

From this time forward in the last years of the nineteenth century, Hardy spent his time and energy writing and publishing verse, with his first volume of poetry, *Wessex Poems*, appearing in 1898. The poems contain many of Hardy's characteristic attitudes and beliefs, a number of them being anecdotes illustrating the perversity of fate and the ironies of coincidence. Long impatient with the constraints of serialized fiction and by now having become rich from the success of his novels, Hardy continued to write poetry and short stories. He also wrote an epic-drama of the Napoleonic Wars, *The Dynasts*, which came out in three parts between 1903 and 1908. While spending more and more time at Max Gate, he received a steady stream of visitors, including the Prince of Wales. Though he was offered knighthood, he declined. In 1910, however, he did accept the

Order of Merit, the highest honor that can be paid to an English author. Fifteen months following the death of his first wife, Emma, he married Florence Emily Dugdale, on November 27, 1912, a teacher approximately forty years his junior. Nevertheless, despite his remarrying, many of his poems provide a powerful expression to his sense of loss with the death of Emma Hardy. On January 11, 1928, Hardy died at Max Gate at the age of eighty-seven.

"Hap"

Written in 1865, "Hap" is a sonnet, a fourteen-line poem, patterned after the Spenserian and Shakespearean model. The basic format is that of a poem in three parts, the first two divisions are quatrains (stanzas of four lines) which present a particular issue or problem, followed by a sestet (the last six lines of sonnet) which contains a turn of thought and response to the issue presented. The speaker in "Hap" is experiencing a crisis of faith, struggling to find the divine motivation for an indifferent universe, a world ruled merely by chance.

The first two stanzas set forth the speaker's plaintive questions to a cold and detached supreme being, while the third and last stanza results in a different perspective, a resigned acceptance of cosmic indifference. The speaker in the poem cries out against an indifferent universe, cruel in its insensitivity. Indeed, the title of the poem itself provides an important key to our understanding the speaker's struggle to find an answer to the inexplicable. The word hap itself contains a dual meaning, referring to a chance or accidental occurrence which can be either an expression of good luck or misfortune. Thus, by its very title, "Hap" presents an inherent tension within the poem.

However, the speaker here must decide between an indifferent universe or a vengeful god who strives against mankind and feeds on human suffering: "'Thou suffering thing, / Know that thy sorrow is my ecstasy, / That thy love's loss is my hate's profiting!'" Hardy's language creates a heightened sense of a spiritual struggle with an inexplicably cruel divinity, as "ecstasy" refers to a trance or rapture that accompanies religious or mystical inspiration. It can also be used as a term for poetic frenzy and seems apt for the highly dramatic speaker here, one equally preoccupied by his rhetorical engagement with an enigmatic divinity as he is with his spiritual crisis. The problem for the speaker is to find some way to understand the motivation of a "Powerfuller" one who controls man's destiny. J.O. Bailey attributes Hardy's reading of Darwin's theory of natural selection in *The Origin of Species*, as being synonymous with the idea of mere accident in a meaningless universe and a disassociated God. Martin Seymour-Smith, however, maintains that the crisis expressed in "Hap" relates to Hardy's pre-Darwinian understanding and is directly influenced by his reading of Aeschylus. As evidence for this, Seymour-Smith cites an entry Hardy made in his diary in May 1865: "The world does not despise us; it only neglects us." In either case, we know Hardy was doubtful that a benevolent God governed the world. The speaker's desperate attempt for an answer is doomed to failure by the very first words he speaks—"If but"—because his desired interlocutor is absent.

In the first stanza the speaker fervently wishes for a cruel divinity, a vengeful God whom he imagines is looking down on the earth, mocking the anguish he inflicts on mankind. He desperately wants to hold this spiteful deity accountable for his supposed evil actions. The speaker's first wish is for a response from just such an imagined deity to confirm the possibility that man's deepest anguish is heaven's absolute joy. The speaker is pleading for a rational explanation for the suffering caused by an indifferent divinity.

In the second stanza, the speaker's rhetoric becomes increasingly rigorous as he takes his imaginary struggle with a vengeful god a step further to a direct confrontation. "Then would I bear it, clench myself, and die, / Steeled by the sense of ire unmerited." The speaker is indignant and provocative, and language he would use to strive with this Powerfuller being bears a similarity to the masculine rhetoric of the seventeenth-century metaphysical poets. It is a decidedly rigorous and challenging idiom in which the speaker will fortify and "clench" himself into accepting this terrible injustice. What matters most is that he receives a response, even if it confirms his worst anxieties. But, as previously noted, his confrontation with a vengeful god is destined to fail because it is predicated on a response he "fashioned" in the first stanza and, more importantly, because this Powerfuller is inaccessible to him. When he conceives an answer from this powerful entity, it is a response borne wholly of his own imagination. "Know that thy sorrow is my ecstasy."

In the third stanza, an important shift takes place when the speaker acknowledges the impossibility of his desired dialogue because his imagined Powerfuller does not exist. Instead, the speaker will first answer his own question concerning the reason for human suffering, "How arrives it joy lies slain, / And why unblooms the best hope ever sown?" and, having done so, will be able to retract his former bravado. His retraction begins with the notion of the "unblooming" of hope, a rhetorical gesture of extreme exertion on the part of the speaker. The idea of "unblooming" is fraught with implication both in terms of the crisis he is attempting to resolve and the means by which he is articulating this very difficult task. To "unbloom" is not merely a term of neglect but, rather, a matter of undoing something that will require great skill and effort underscoring the speaker's passionate investment. The idea of "unblooming" also continues the conceit of being "steeled by the sense of ire" in the prior stanza, for the word "bloom," from the Old English *blŏma*, refers to a mass of steel or other metal hammered into a thick bar for further working. It is also an expression of Hardy's notion of a mechanized universe of chance happenings.

Having given up the rhetorical struggle with an absent opponent, the speaker is finally able to attribute all misfortune to Crass Casualty and the games of "dicing Time." All mortal suffering is brought about by "purblind Doomsters," judges who have decided his fate long ago. Indeed, the universe of "Hap" is a mechanical one without purpose, indifferent to man's suffering and one devoid of hope, redemption or transcendent potential.

"Hap"

[Joanna Cullen Brown is the editor of *Figures in a Wessex
Landscape: Thomas Hardy's Picture of English Country Life*
(1987) and *Let Me Enjoy the Earth: Thomas Hardy and Nature*
(1990). In the following excerpt from her book, Brown
discusses the rhetoric of the "mechanical universe" in "Hap."]

HAP

If but some vengeful god would call to me
From up the sky, and laugh: "Thou suffering thing,
Know that thy sorrow is my ecstasy,
That thy love's loss is my hate's profiting!"

Then would I bear it, clench myself, and die,
Steeled by the sense of ire unmerited;
Half-eased in that a Powerfuller than I
Had willed and meted me the tears I shed.

But not so. How arrives it joy lies slain,
And why unblooms the best hope ever sown?
—Crass Casualty obstructs the sun and rain,
And dicing Time for gladness casts a moan....
These purblind Doomsters had as readily strown
Blisses about my pilgrimage as pain.

1866
16 Westbourne Park Villas

These tightly-knit lines of argument do not at first reading yield
their treasures. There seems nothing new in the theme of the
gods sporting with humankind—until it is turned, on the pivotal
"But not so", to Hardy's own individual angle: it is the chance,
random nature of life's buffetings that hurts, the offering of joy

and its pointless, unheeding withholding. Diction and rhythm double the meaning.

> How arrives it joy lies slain,
> And why unblooms the best hope ever sown?

The hard, harsh teeth-clenched words of stanza two unfold at once into a larger tone of long vowels and soft final consonants— slain, sown, blooms; the human, personal voice and question sounding not only against the fixed metrical frame of the sonnet, but against the rigid voice of a mechanical universe. ("Mechanic" is a recurrent Hardyan term of abuse.) The answer reflects that "mechanic speech" and "mechanic gear" and those "mechanic repetitions" in its mouthful of stressed, crunching consonants "Cráss Cásualty obstrúcts"—set in immediate contrast to the simple basics of life, the sun and rain, which sing themselves. Hardy's typical negative "unblooms" is particularly poignant in the way it holds fruitful promise before our eyes only to deny it. His "dicing Time" has a mincing cruelty quite apart from its meaning; the "Doomsters" (Middle English, a *judge*) are the last people who should be "purblind": the discrepancies of life are everywhere in the poem. Here is one who is prepared to regard life as a pilgrimage, with all its overtones of purpose and stoicism; yet the slap in the face comes just as smartly. The life is strewn with the withered buds of a happiness that has never blossomed. The last word is pain.

"Hap", dated and placed in London in 1866, shows astonishing mastery of its medium, and Hardy's own idiom already clearly developed. Its pain and anger, so intensely felt, point to some of his suffering as a young man. By the turn of the century, when *Poems of the Past and Present* were published (November 1901), the dozen poems put together which all survey "God", "Nature", and humanity's lot are mostly less angry than exquisitely sad. (…)

Hardy is a giant of metrical, rhyming, and verbal variation. Dennis Taylor reckons that in 1089 poems, he uses 799 metrical forms, of which he has invented 629. (He compares this with

Swinburne's 420 different forms, Tennyson's 240, and Robert Browning's 200.[2] This fact is impressive; but this is not the place to burrow into the lengthy tables furnished by research students who have valiantly examined the stresses and rhymes of every two-line, three-line, four-line, and up to 26-line stanza which Hardy wrote. The important thing about his craftsmanship is not so much what he did (though this can be fascinating), as why and how he did it—in his pursuit of reality, to use every possible way of shaping and extending meaning. Every gift and layer of experience—like his musical ear and his intelligent study of the classics—added to his awareness of the power of metre, or measure, to "carry a rational content", to contribute essentially to what he was trying to say.

We have seen how Hardy, tongue in cheek, used hymnal Long Measure to raise the ghost of morality in "The Ruined Maid". More seriously, many of his most agnostic poems are ironically cast in the (even more) Common Measure of hymns of faith—his recognition that tension and paradox are at the heart of life. This recognition is one of the most important elements in his poetry; and he used metre, the language of stresses and speech rhythms, to express it. His rhythms image all the rhythms of life: the rhythms of our inner life of thought and spirit, and the conflicting rhythms of the universe, which at times synchronise but usually end in a clash of dissonance and mistiming. So the metrical framework can represent the straitjacket of fate, time and circumstance against which the human heart bursts in its own rhythms of longing and suffering. "Hap" is a good illustration because it is cast in the tight mould of the sonnet and the iambic pentameter. The rhythm we know so well in a line like: "Whĕn I | cŏnsí | dĕr hów | m̆y líght | iš spént |" is broken, in "Hap", by the harsh stresses of lines like:

Thăt thy loʹve's lóss iš mý háte's prófitiňg

—the stresses of our normal speech which are required to express the conflicting demands of "my" and "thy". "Hap" shows the human voice responding in all its individuality to the inhuman, "mechanic" rigidity of the universe.

—Joanna Cullen Brown. *A Journey Into Thomas Hardy's Poetry*.
London: W.H. Allen & Co Plc (1989): 194–96 and 272–3.

DENNIS TAYLOR ON THE LANGUAGE OF PERSONIFICATION

[Dennis Taylor is the author of *Hardy's Literary Language and Victorian Philology* (1993) and *Hardy's Metres and Victorian Prosody: With a Metrical Appendix of Hardy's Stanza Forms* (1988). In the following excerpt, Taylor discusses the language of personification in "Hap."]

In 'Hap' the speaker tries to find a language to portray reality as it really is. He tries to see past the personifications ('If but some vengeful god would call to me'), the equivalences ('thy love's loss is my hate's profiting'), and cause–effect categories ('a Powerfuller than I | Had willed and meted me the tears I shed') of anthropomorphic views.

If but some vengeful god would call to me
From up the sky, and laugh: 'Thou suffering thing,
Know that thy sorrow is my ecstasy,
That thy love's loss is my hate's profiting!'

Then would I bear it, clench myself, and die,
Steeled by the sense of ire unmerited;
Half-eased in that a Powerfuller than I
Had willed and meted me the tears I shed.

But not so. How arrives it joy lies slain,
And why unblooms the best hope ever sown?
—Crass Casualty obstructs the sun and rain,
And dicing Time for gladness casts a moan....
These purblind Doomsters had as readily strown
Blisses about my pilgrimage as pain.

The speaker hopes to discern a reality that stands outside all assumptions of archaic order. But he remains trapped in the language of personifications ('dicing Time'), equivalences ('for gladness casts a moan'), and cause–effect ('How arrives it?'). 'Hap' tries to name a reality beyond God; but the names found for the new reality—*Hap* ('arch.'), *Casualty* ('obs.'), *Doomsters* ('arch.')—illustrate the anachronism in which the search for understanding is caught. Trying to express that reality, the 'nothing that is' which undoes rational expectations, he must use *Casualty* in a grammatical form which contradicts its meaning: 'Crass Casualty obstructs the sun'. ('Natural Selection' was a famous contemporary case of a self-contradictory solecism, an anachronism imposed belatedly on blind natural processes.) Empson, a formidable critic of Hardy, says of 'Hap': 'This sonnet is very badly written, so badly that it cannot be admired at all, except for a kind of hammered-out sincerity.' But the defence of sincerity, a traditional one, does Hardy little service. Another defence is, of course, possible, that such a poem satirizes a dramatic speaker. But Empson sensed that the poem is closer to Hardy's ingrained habits of speech than a purely dramatistic approach would allow. Hardy and speaker converge in a common sense of the enmeshing of consciousness in a complex language system. We must see the poem in the rich context of the philological age in which it was written. Interestingly, the poem may have been partly inspired by Hardy's reading in Nuttall's *Standard Pronouncing Dictionary*, signed by Hardy in 1865; among the various words marked are *Deemster, dempster,* and *doomsman* (see Appendix 3). Also in his 1865 *Studies, Specimens &c.* notebook Hardy copied Scott's use of 'had happed' (*Marmion,* iv, line 457), and from *The Golden Treasury* 'happed' and 'haply', the latter from Shakespeare's 'When in disgrace with fortune and men's eyes'. He also underlined 'heavie hap' and 'chaunst' in his 1865 Spenser and 'hapless' in 'Lycidas' in his 1865 Milton. 'Hap' has much philological history behind it.[9]

NOTE

9. *CPW*, i. 10; Empson, 'The Voice of the Underdog', review of Wayne Booth's *Rhetoric of Irony, New York Review of Books* (12 June 1975), 38; Spenser, I.

I. 27; iii. 20; see Hynes on the poem: 'his abstractions sometimes get in the way of his things' (p. 5). 'Hap' (1866) was probably inspired in part by Browning's 'Caliban upon Setebos' (1864). 'Caliban' illustrates the growth of an anthropomorphic theology even as he mimics a God who does not care, as though God were to say: 'Well, as the chance were, this might take or else | Not take my fancy: I might hear his cry, | And give the mankin three sound legs for one, | or pluck the other off.' (II. 90–3).

—Dennis Taylor. *Hardy's Literary Language and Victorian Philology.* Oxford and New York: Oxford University Press (1993): 300–301.

Robert Langbaum on Hardy's Late Romanticism

[Robert Langbaum is the author of *The Word from Below: Essays on Modern Literature and Culture* (1987) and *The Poetry of Experience: The Dramatic Monologue in Modern Literary Tradition* (1985). In the following excerpt, Langbaum discusses "Hap" and "Neutral Tones" as examples of Hardy's late romanticism.]

It is not clear whether Hardy's imagism developed from his own objective realism (already evident in 'On the Departure Platform', 1909), or whether he was influenced by the Imagist poets. He appears to have read volumes sent him by Ezra Pound in 1920–1 and by Amy Lowell in 1922, but his responses to these young Imagists do not suggest influence (*Letters*, VI: 49, 77–8, 186). The phrase in his last volume, 'Just neutral-tinted haps' ('He Never Expected Much', III: 225), explains what he always aimed to convey, so that the neutrality characteristic of imagism was incipient in his earliest poems 'Neutral Tones' and 'Hap'. Hardy's objective realism or metonymy is more characteristic of his poetry than are metaphor and symbol.[21]

If we apply to Hardy Eliot's remark about Kipling's variety, we find that as poet Hardy exhibits even more variety than Kipling, in that he passes not only from form to form and subject to subject but also from level to level. For he mixes with humorous verse and melodramatic balladry poems that are serious philosophically and others that are in the full sense 'poetry'.

Yet we do not feel in reading through a Hardy volume the

assured pitch of intensity that we feel with indubitably major poets or the equally assured lightness of versifiers. Hardy's variousness can be entertaining if we are alive to his shifts of tone, otherwise we may become impatient with his skilful ballads and narratives because our standards have been determined by the greater depths of emotion and psychological insights offered in the major poems. (…)

Instead of romantic projection, Hardy often uses the traditional devices of allegory and personification to make nature yield meaning. In 'The Darkling Thrush', the landscape becomes 'The [Nineteenth] Century's corpse outleant' (I: 187). In 'Hap' (1866), Hardy realises that 'Crass Casualty' would strew 'blisses' in my path as readily as the 'pain' I encounter (I: 10) so that design of any kind, even malevolent design, would be a consolation. Although a later poem 'The Subalterns' (1901) makes the opposite point—that life seems less grim when the speaker realises that Cold, Sickness and Death are like himself helpless agents of natural laws (I: 155)—both poems insist on nature's indifference. Here and elsewhere Hardy's blatant anthropomorphism, as compared to Wordsworth's gentle animation of nature, indicates how utterly *non*-anthropomorphic nature really is. Only the self-referentiality of Hardy's artificial rhetoric can convey the meaning of meaninglessness.

'Hap' and 'The Subalterns' belong to a class of poems cast as dialogues among personified natural forces. The theological purport of such dialogues on nature's indifference ('God-Forgotten' is another example) precludes Wordsworthian feelings of nature's meaning that might emerge from realistic renditions of nature and that do emerge from the few poems where Hardy does treat nature realistically. These theological dialogues do not in my opinion rank among Hardy's best poems, because divorced from sensation, but we could not do without them because they are so Hardyan. What does poignantly shine through these poems, amid the cosmic indifference and blundering, is man's *humanity*, for they show man as more rational and moral than the force that created him. Hardy never reduces man to an automaton, not even in *The Dynast*, which announces its determinism.

NOTE

21. See Patricia O'Neill, 'Thomas Hardy: Poetics of a Postromantic', *Victorian Poetry*, 27:2 (Summer 1989), 129–45. Although Paul Zietlow, in *Moments of Vision: The Poetry of Thomas Hardy* (Cambridge: Harvard University Press, 1974), shows how Hardy's realism sometimes opens out to epiphany, Hardy is not notably an epiphanic poet.

—Robert Langbaum. *Thomas Hardy in Our Time*. New York: St. Martin's Press, Inc. (1995): 39 and 45–6.

PAUL ZEITLOW ON THE DRAMATIC POSTURING OF THE SPEAKER

[Paul Zeitlow is the author of "The Ascending Concerns of *The Ring and the Book*: Reality, Moral Vision, and Salvation" (1987) and "Heard but Unheeded: The Songs of Callicles of Mathew Arnold's 'Empedocles on Etna'" (1983). In the excerpt below from "On Poetic Art," Zietlow discusses the dramatic posturing of the speaker in "Hap."]

Any attempt to understand Hardy's poetry must therefore begin with an acknowledgment of the distinctiveness of each poem. A comparison of poems as similar as "Discouragement," "Hap," and "The Sleepwalker" illustrates the variety of voices and identities in Hardy's poetry. All are sonnets; two of them, "Hap" and "Discouragement," were written in the same period, the mid 1860s; and all are pessimistic in outlook. Yet in each poem quite different voices and quite different shades of meaning can be identified.

There is a remarkable different between the objectivity of the speaker in "Discouragement" and the self-dramatizing posturing of the speaker in "Hap," a poem of the same period.

The speaker begins by positing what appears to be the most desperate metaphysical possibility of all—not simply a malign god but a "vengeful" one, a god not merely ill-intentioned but who bears a grudge that can only be satisfied by the speaker's suffering. He imagines this god as speaking in words dripping hatred, bitterness, and contempt, expressing his pleasure in the speaker's pain. Yet he explains that he could accept such a deity, because then he could die "steeled," "half-eased." But he would not merely die; he would "bear it, clench [him]self, and die," like a hero, not merely having suffered but having borne the suffering and endured. He would die only after a final defiant, self-defining gesture–a clenching of the fist, a hugging of the body, or a doubling up in self-enclosure.

The sestet describes the speaker's reality, which for him is even more desperate than what he had imagined: "Crass Casualty," "dicing Time," and the "purblind Doomsters" have blighted his life. The question arises as to why he could not still bear it, clench himself, and die. His fate is still unmerited; he is still the victim of a force more powerful than himself. The answer is that he craves to be the object of specific ire, the victim of special intention. He imagines God as speaking to himself alone, not to all mankind. He prefers to think of himself on center stage, as not merely the leading actor but the only actor in a drama of vengeful injustice meted out by the all-powerful on a hero who endures, chooses his own moment of death, and refuses to be broken. The speaker elevates his whole life to high drama. He has experienced sorrow, lost love and shed tears, felt joy, and harbored "the *best* hope ever sown"; the course of his life has been a "pilgrimage." His phrasing relies on contrasting extremes, antithetical absolutes: "sorrow"—"ecstasy," "love's loss"—"hate's profiting," "gladness"—"moan," "blisses"—"pain." The final lines, which are clogged with consonants, syntactically contorted, and punctuated with metrically stressed plosives, employ Hardy's harsh style to express intensities of bitterness, hatred, contempt and self-pity: "These purblind Doomsters had as readily strown / Blisses about my pilgrimage as pain." This is one of those poems in which the distance between the speaker and the author is difficult to gauge. Yet in my judgment no irony is intended in the speaker's view of himself, despite the overt self dramatization. The poem produces an effect of exaggeration without parody; the reader is aware of ego, not egomania. The speaker's mode resembles the posturing of romantic heroism, in the tradition of Heathcliff, Manfred and Eustacia Vye.

—Paul Zeitlow. *Moments of Vision: The Poetry of Thomas Hardy*. Cambridge, MA: Harvard University Press (1974): 58–61.

CRITICAL ANALYSIS OF
"Neutral Tones"

Dated 1867, "Neutral Tones" was written during Hardy's first visit to London and the anonymous woman to whom it is addressed is believed to be Eliza Nicholls. At the time Hardy first met Eliza in 1863, she was in the service as a lady's maid at the house of barrister near Westbourne Park Villas. Later that same year, Eliza left the district and in 1865 returned to her father's home in Findon, the location of "Neutral Tones."

Similar to the rhetoric of "Hap," "Neutral Tones" continues the theme of a world in which God has absented himself, with a critical difference. While "Hap" refers only to a divine power as a cruelly indifferent Powerfuller, "Neutral Tones" portrays a world in which God is now absent. Furthermore, and equally as important, that abandonment is accompanied by a severe rebuke from God, and is expressed in terms of a profound loss. However, the loss presented in "Neutral Tones" is also about the speaker's grievous disappointment in love as he speaks to an anonymous woman. The title of the poem is important because two different meanings of "neutral" are at play—there is both a resignation on the part of its despondent speaker that the struggle both with God and the woman are now over and that the world now lies in ruin, both colorless and utterly devoid of hope.

The first stanza describes a pond in winter, a desolate and lifeless landscape made all the more stark by a colorless sun spreading white light on a barren soil. "And a few leaves lay on the starving sod; /—They had fallen from an ash, and were gray." And the speaker is very quick to point out that this tragic state is the result of God having forsaken this world, a loss made all the more terrible in that it is accompanied by a severe rebuke from the Almighty, "as though chidden of God."

With God's love removed from the world, the speaker makes an easy transition in the second stanza where he tells us of the dejection he feels over the loss of love from a woman, the one whom he is addressing. "Your eyes on me were as eyes that rove

/ Over tedious riddles of years ago." Thinking back on his lover's gaze, the speaker imagines her tired and bored with him and yet, curiously, beyond that very same indifference, to the point of being troubled—all that the word tediousness denotes. It would seem this disagreeable boredom is a wish to be done with her long-standing attempt to understand him, that the answer is not worth the effort she has already expended. Furthermore, inasmuch as a riddle is the name for a mechanical device which separates corn from chaff, and in traditional literary terms good poetry from bad, the problem of neutrality here is the inability to make the necessary distinctions in order to find truth in a mechanical world. The speaker imagines that she perceives any attempt to establish a meaningful communication with him a wasted endeavor, a hopelessly inconclusive game. "And some words played between us to and fro / On which lost the more by our love."

By the third stanza, a resigned melancholia has set in as the speaker describes his all but absent lover, the only part of this dreary world that contains the necessary vitality to be rendered lifeless. "The smile on your mouth was the deadest thing / Alive enough to have strength to die." Having pronounced his lover dead to himself and to the world, his anger becomes even more intensified as he turns his attention to the God-forsaken world he inhabits and reads future misfortune in the landscape he observes. "And a grin of bitterness swept thereby / Like an ominous bird a-wing."

Finally, the fourth and final stanza of "Neutral Tones" is an articulation of all that the speaker has learned of love, both human and divine, a despondent retrospective that yields a message of total despair, "keen lessons that love deceives." Both the posture of the speaker and the world on which he comments is devoid of any distinction, a fact which ironically creates enormous distress rather than complete boredom. His tone is one of resignation as the painful memories are etched in his memory. "Your face, and the God-curst sun, and a tree, / And a pond edged with grayish leaves."

CRITICAL VIEWS ON
"Neutral Tones"

SAMUEL HYNES ON THE CHARACTERISTICS OF HARDY'S MATURE STYLE

[Samuel Hynes is the author of *The Edwardian Turn of Mind* (1968); *A War Imagined: The First World War and English Culture* (1991); and *The Growing Seasons: An American Boyhood Before the War* (2003). In the following excerpt, Hynes discusses "Neutral Tones" as an excellent example of an early poem exhibiting the characteristics of Hardy's mature style.]

"Neutral Tones" we immediately recognize as a fine poem in Hardy's most characteristic style: the plain but not quite colloquial language, the hard, particular, colorless images, the slightly odd stanza-form, the dramatic handling of the occasion, the refusal to resolve the issue—all these we have seen in Hardy's best poems. The poem does not distort the syntax of ordinary speech nor draw on exotic sources of diction, yet it is obviously *not* ordinary speech—only Hardy would say "a grin of bitterness swept thereby / Like an ominous bird a-wing," or "wrings with wrong," or would describe a winter sun as "God-curst."

The details of the setting of "Neutral Tones" are not, strictly speaking, metaphorical, but they combine to create a mood which is appropriate both to a dismal winter day and to the end of love, and in this way love and weather, the emotions and the elements, symbolize each other in a way that is common to many of Hardy's best poems ("Weathers," "The Darkling Thrush," and "During Wind and Rain," for example) and to some moving passages in the novels as well (*Far From the Madding Crowd* is full of scenes constructed in this way).

"Neutral Tones" is an excellent example of Hardy's mature style, drawn from his earliest productive period; I cite it as evidence that he did not develop through new styles as he grew older (as Yeats did), but that he simply learned to use better what he already had. In the poem we recognize and acknowledge one man's sense of the world;, if it is somber, it is also precise, and the precision lends authority to the vision. In "Revulsion," on the other hand, the pessimism is a case not proven; the poem offers nothing to persuade us of the speaker's right to speak as he does. In the 1860–70 decade there are many poems like "Revulsion," but there is only one "Neutral Tones." Hardy was not Hardy very often.

—Samuel Hynes. *The Pattern of Hardy's Poetry*. Chapel Hill, N.C.: The University of North Carolina Press (1961): 136–37.

J.O. BAILEY ON "NEUTRAL TONES" AS A POEM ABOUT RUINS

[J.O. Bailey is the author of "Ancestral Voices in *Jude the Obscure*" (1972) and "Heredity as Villain in the Poetry and Fiction of Thomas Hardy" (1970). In the following excerpt from his book, Bailey discusses "Neutral Tones" as a poem about ruins—passionate love, disillusion, and bitterness.]

"Neutral tones" has the effect of an etching in steel by a man trained in drawing the ruins of old churches, as Hardy was. The ruins of the poem are those of passionate love, disillusioned, embittered, and etched on the memory in images of nature in winter. The movement of the poem is from the scene as it scored its images upon the mind anesthetized by despair, to the contemplation of these images in their universal meanings— from a sun whitened "as though chidden of God and leaves "fallen from an ash," to a "God-curst sun" and the dead leaves lying there. The ash tree (with its suggestion of ashes in the name) was an ancient symbol of happiness. But its once-green leaves have decayed into the "neutral" grayish.

The intensity of this etching and the particularity of its images suggest that it presents Hardy's actual experience. The pond seems the same as that treated in "At Rushy-Pond." Deacon and Coleman have suggested that the poem presents a crisis in Hardy's love for Tryphena Sparks. The poem is dated 1867 and, according to Purdy,[1] was written at Hardy's lodgings in London in that year, before he returned to Higher Bockhampton and met Tryphena. "But," say Deacon and Coleman, "perhaps this indicates not the year in which it was composed but the year in which Hardy and Tryphena became lovers, a year of hopefulness at first, but one which led to the despair of 1871."[2] Such evasive dating, perhaps to conceal the fact, is a possibility.

In his novels Hardy often summarized a disaster by presenting the scene etched on a character's memory. In *Desperate Remedies*, Cytherea faints when her father falls from a scaffold; as she recovers, the scene is etched on her mind: "... her eyes caught sight of the southwestern sky, and, without heeding, saw white sunlight shining in shaft-like lines from a rift in a slaty cloud.... Even after that time any mental agony brought less vividly to Cytherea's mind the scene from the Town Hall windows than sunlight streaming in shaft-like lines." (Chapter I, 3.) When Elfride, in *A Pair of Blue Eyes*, confesses to Knight her former love for Stephen Smith, "The word fell like a bolt, and the very land and sky seemed to suffer.... The scene was engraved for years on Knight's eye: the dead and brown stubble, the weeds among it, the distant belt of beeches shutting out the view of the house, the leaves of which were now red and sick to death." (Chapter XXXIV.) On discovering the loss of his sheep, Gabriel in *Far from the Madding Crowd* "raised his head, and wondering what he could do, listlessly surveyed the scene. By the outer margin of the pit was an oval pond, and over it hung the attenuated skeleton of a chrome-yellow moon.... The pool glittered like a dead man's eye.... All this Oak saw and remembered." (Chapter V.)

NOTES

1. *Thomas Hardy: A Bibliographical Study*, p. 98.
2. *Providence and Mr. Hardy*, p. 82.

—J.O. Bailey. *The Poetry of Thomas Hardy: A Handbook and Commentary.* Chapel Hill, N.C.: The University of North Carolina Press (1970): 55–6.

[Trevor Johnson is the author of *Thomas Hardy* (1968) and *Joseph Andrews by Henry Fielding (A Critical Guide)* (1987). In the following excerpt from his book, Johnson discusses "Neutral Tones" as a poem giving way to hopelessness and disillusion.]

Neutral Tones (9/ALL/H/*)

The very first reviewer to address himself to Hardy's verse paused in his wholesale demolition of *Wessex Poems* for the *Saturday Review* in 1899 to allow this poem as an instance of Hardy's 'mature strength'; Middleton Murry in 1919 unhesitatingly termed it 'major poetry' and in 1929 F.R. Leavis included it in his, to say the least ungenerous, allocation of a 'dozen or so poems' on which he perceived Hardy's 'rank as a major poet' to rest. Many critics have echoed them so I must hope not to appear merely perverse if I enter a few caveats to the inclusion of *Neutral Tones*—fine poem as it undoubtedly is—in the ranks of Hardy's major masterpieces.

It is pointless to speculate on the identity of the woman involved; the location on the other hand is very probably the pond on the heath near Puddletown which gives its name to another poem *At Rushy Pond* (680/D/*). Though less successful, this exhibits some interesting thematic correspondences with *Neutral Tones*, and its second stanza is quite as brilliantly visual as the first of what was probably a companion piece. (*At Rushy Pond* is undated and was published much later.)

The intensely realized setting is, of course, what first takes the reader's eye, a feature aptly compared by J.O. Bailey to 'an etching in steel'. For the poem is wholly devoid of colour and movement; its wintry stillness and silence an integral part of its mood, the inanition which succeeds a once passionate love gone irrevocably sour. The lovers have nothing significant to say to each other, the landscape has nothing to say to them of spring or summer. We cannot usefully talk about 'background' here; *where it happened* is as important as what took place in the anguished impression which memory holds.

The stanza form is simple; rhymed quatrains with an internal couplet, but there are some subtle variations in stress and rhythmic pattern which can best be seen by comparing the last lines of each stanza. Apart from the rather mannered *chidden of God*, the language is similarly unaffected for the most part. There are certainly some reminiscences of D.G. Rossetti (especially of *Willowwood III* and, thematically perhaps, of *The Woodspurge*), but the echoes are quite faint and probably unconscious.

It is difficult to fault the first two stanzas either for economy or clarity of expression; I am, however, a little less happy with the third. The trope on *deadest* and *die* has an ingenuity foreign to Hardy at his best; such verbal sleights-of-hand, impressive at a first reading, come to feel meretricious on further acquaintance. Nor is it quite clear to what the conjunction *thereby* refers. Again, the closing simile—aside from the fact that the *ominous bird* has a whiff of cliché about it—is not altogether convincing. Does a *grin* in fact suggest a bird in flight? I think the whole stanza is something of an elaboration, and the return in the last to the directness and precision of the first two reinforces this impression. The adjective *keen* with its double sense of 'eager' and 'painful', the assured word-play of *wrings with wrong* (where the homophone 'rings' gives 'surrounds' as well as 'twists') and the telling return to the opening, with the brilliant 'turn' of *God-curst sun*, perverting that primal source of warmth and light into a malign presence; all these are impressive aspects of a poem which, one might say, gives a voice to mute despair and disillusion. Overall, *Neutral Tones* displays a diamond-hard, if cold, brilliance. But it is monochromatic; to place it beside one of the *Poems of 1912–13* is to see that there is a precociousness, an inevitable immaturity in it, which precludes our rating it with Hardy's greatest verse.

—Trevor Johnson. *A Critical Introduction to the Poems of Thomas Hardy*. New York: St. Martin's Press, Inc. (1991): 178–9.

[Dennis Taylor is the author of *Hardy's Literary Language and Victorian Philology* (1993) and *Hardy's Metres and Victorian Prosody: With a Metrical Appendix of Hardy's Stanza Forms* (1988). In the following excerpt, Taylor discusses "Neutral Tones" as a word game in which Hardy plays on the difference between older and current formation of words.]

'Neutral Tones' is a poem about 'keen lessons' and 'riddles'.

We stood by a pond that winter day,
And the sun was white, as though chidden of God,
And a few leaves lay on the starving sod;
  —They had fallen from an ash, and were gray.

Your eyes on me were as eyes that rove
Over tedious riddles of years ago;
And some words played between us to and fro
  On which lost the more by our love.

The smile on your face was the deadest thing
Alive enough to have strength to die;
And a grin of bitterness swept thereby
  Like an ominous bird a-wing....

Since then, keen lessons that love deceives,
And wrings with wrong, have shaped to me
Your face, and the God-curst sun, and a tree,
  And a pond edged with grayish leaves.

The speaker tries to understand why love has died between him and his lover. But though the past crisis shapes his later years, he cannot understand its nature. The poem's opening image has an oddly empty clarity about it, like a wide open unseeing eye. Things are stated clearly and yet offer no ultimate illumination, only repetition. A 'keen lesson', which is simply repeated, does not educate. To emphasize this point, Hardy revised 'riddles solved years ago' to 'riddles of years ago'. The riddles remain unsolved. An additional problem is that as the event is repeated in the mind which seeks to understand it, the event changes slightly. Indeed, the very language by which the event is described changes as one uses it. To illustrate this point, an 'identical' scene is described differently in the first and last stanzas, as if to say that even as we find words to describe our recollection, the past is always changing for us, however slightly. And so also with the words we must use to recapture that past. The poem is full of plays on the difference between older and current formations of words. For example, *a-wing* versus the more normalized alive, 'chidden *of* God' versus 'riddles *of* years ago', *thereby* (in 'arch. and dial.' sense of 'by there') versus 'by a pond'. '*Wrings* with *wrong*' plays with the ancient etymology of *wrong* from the past participle of wrings which is a rare intransitive verb. (This etymology is discussed as an example of a word's spelling revealing its etymology, in Trench's *On the Study of Words*, 202.) *Keen, lessons, riddles*, have an interesting etymological history related to the meanings 'know' or 'read'. In this poem, readings become tedious riddles, omens (as in 'ominous bird') are never clarified and end in ellipses, lessons become keen and painful repetitions, scenes become static shapes, tones become neutral, and chiding (from another metaphorical God) becomes a dark and empty curse. Words 'play between' them, 'play on' endlessly, and are 'played on', in the multiple reading of lines 7–8. The speaker's present understanding of himself is like a language riddle, a keen lesson whose origins and consequences are shrouded in mystery.[24]

Thus Trench wrote:

> When a word entirely refuses to give up the secret of its origin, it can be regarded in no other light but as a riddle which no one has succeeded in solving, a lock of which no one has found the key— but still a riddle which has a solution, a lock for which there is a key, though now, it may be, irrecoverably lost. (*Study*, 154)

The philological riddle is pointedly connected by Hardy with the emotional riddle. In the two conflicting readings of line 8, words speak (and debate which of them 'lost the more'), but do not offer clarifying illumination, and so make the lovers lose all 'the more'.

NOTE

24. *CPW*, i. 13; also see Doherty and Taylor. Charles Tomlinson, in 'Ritornello' (*The Flood* (Oxford, 1981)) plays on the etymology of *wrong*: 'Wrong has a twisty look like wrung misprinted.' Into his *Studies, Specimens &c.* notebook, Hardy copied 'chidden' from *The Golden Treasury* (no. xvii, 'Beauty sat bathing').

—Dennis Taylor. *Hardy's Literary Language and Victorian Philology.* Oxford and New York: Oxford University Press (1993): 275–77.

ROBERT LANGBAUM ON HARDY'S MODERNISM

[Robert Langbaum is the author of *The Word from Below: Essays on Modern Literature and Culture* (1987) and *The Poetry of Experience: The Dramatic Monologue in Modern Literary Tradition* (1985). In the following excerpt, Langbaum discusses "Neutral Tones" as a poem exemplifying Hardy's "new voice," characteristic of and appropriated by the great modernist poets of the twentieth century.]

I spoke earlier of Hardy's importance as an influence on later poets, and this ability to influence comes from his powerful connection with the whole nineteenth-century tradition of British poetry. C. M. Bowra rightly called him 'the most representative British poet between Tennyson and Yeats'.[22] The great modernist poets *thought* they were repudiating their nineteenth-century predecessors (Pound's homage to Browning and Yeats's to Blake and Shelley are exceptions), whereas Hardy revised the nineteenth-century poets while still admiring them, even perhaps considering them greater poets than he. Hardy's poetry exhibits many voices, but the voice we discern as modern often derives from realistic revisions of romantic rhetoric and themes—especially revisions of the romanticists he admired most, Wordsworth and Shelley. His most important Victorian influences—Browning and Swinburne—are assimilated without much critical comment. Hardy may be said to have passed on the nineteenth-century tradition in a form usable by twentieth-century poets.

A good example of Hardy's new voice is 'Neutral Tones', a poem written as early as 1867. The first stanza like the title establishes the theme of neutrality, a reaction against romantic colourfulness and significance:

> We stood by a pond that winter day,
> And the sun was white, as though chidden of God,
> And a few leaves lay on the starving sod;
>   —They had fallen from an ash, and were gray.

The stanza addresses the central issue of romantic nature poetry-the pathetic fallacy, the projection into nature of human qualities. The neutrality of Hardy's-landscape suggests, instead, that nature is indifferent and alien.

Hardy's lovers exhibit a love as depleted of value as the landscape: 'And some words played between us to and fro / On which [of us] lost the more by our love'. Their love was valueless, not only now when it is over, but even while it was operative. Yet the landscape oscillates between objective neutrality and deliberately invoked pathetic fallacy. The movement is from 'And the sun was white, as though chidden of God' to the final lines in which the speaker drops 'as though' and speaks simply, in association with the lover's hated face, of 'the God-curst sun' (I: 13). Here and elsewhere Hardy achieves powerful ironies by invoking the pathetic fallacy in order to suggest its inapplicability but also its psychological inevitability—in order to suggest that under the pressure of emotion we conceive nature's neutrality as malevolent. Such oscillation between nature's neutrality and malevolence runs through the poems and novels.

NOTE

22. C.M. Bowra, 'The Lyrical Poetry of Thomas Hardy', *Inspiration and Poetry* (London: Macmillan; New York: St Martin's Press, 1955), p. 220.

—Robert Langbaum. *Thomas Hardy in Our Time*. New York: St. Martin's Press, Inc. (1995): 44–5.

"During Wind and Rain"

Written in 1917, "During Wind and Rain" is both autobiographical and visionary—an imaginative development of scenes in Emma Gifford's (Hardy's first wife) girlhood in Plymouth as they are described in Mrs. Hardy's *Some Recollections*. It is also a poem very much concerned with mutability and the loss of hope and joy. In each of the four stanzas, Hardy weaves a double vision of Emma's happy childhood experiences juxtaposed with his own meditation upon the destruction through the passage of time. Likewise, each stanza begins in a high-spirited optimism as the poet describes scenes of family gatherings and beautiful lawns and trees, yet concludes in a dismal statement of the wreckage wrought by the years as the rose dies and the family name itself becomes effaced by natural erosion. Finally, the stanzas are arranged according to season: an indoor scene in winter, a garden scene in spring; an outdoor breakfast in summer, and a move to a "high new house" during an autumn rainfall.

The first stanza is drawn from Emma's memory of childhood singing when her father would play the violin and her mother would play the piano while singing. It was here that Emma learned to sing in harmony. "They sing their dearest songs– / ... Treble and tenor and bass." It is a time of hope for the future, of individual expression and timeless values, where music has the power to bring people together. But the poet interrupts this domestic scene of peace and contentment as he exclaims that all has fallen to decay. It is the oft-repeated refrain which concludes each stanza: "Ah, no; the years O! / How the sick leaves reel down in throngs!" By reeling down, Hardy wants to convey a tumultuous and noisy interruption, hardly what we would expect from falling leaves, that so rudely disrupts the beautiful sound of voices singing harmoniously.

The second stanza takes place in the garden in springtime. The scene is lush and green, with "creeping moss" while the elder trees are tidily arranged, "making the pathways neat" and opening onto a lovely garden, a peaceful and shady haven.

Emma's girlhood home had fruit trees in bloom, many flower beds, and an aged and great elm tree with garden seats and tables. Yet, for all its loveliness, the poet nevertheless suggests that the garden contains the seeds of its own destruction. In calling it a "gay" garden, Hardy is using a word that describes both a state of happiness and also the dissipation and ruin that can follow such feelings of complete freedom from care. While some critics have attributed these disruptive thoughts as Hardy's commentary on Emma's obsession with her social superiority over her husband, other biographers, such as Seymour-Smith, have a far more benign understanding of her personality and acknowledge that their marriage was, for the most part, a happy one. Whether or not we choose to read these lines as oblique references to Emma Hardy, they do introduce a second level of disruption of the pastoral ideal, the transformation is from the gentle and carefree world of childhood into the troubled world of social pretense, from unfettered happiness to preoccupation and concern with social status. The stanza ends with another violent intrusion from nature with the arrival of the white storm-birds. "Ah, no; the years, the years; / See, the white storm-birds wing across."

The third stanza is also set in the garden, this time during a summertime morning with all gathered at the table, "blithely breakfasting" beneath the shade of the trees. If someone were to look carefully, they are even afforded a faint view of the bay. It is a pastoral scene with the family's pet fowl feeling very much a part of the household and free to mingle. Yet, once again, by describing the family as "blithely" enjoying their morning meal in the very first line of this stanza, the poet is implying that all is not well in this seemingly peaceful setting. Though at first we are made to understand that all assembled are happy, blithely also means to be heedlessly careless while taking no account of consequences, another reminder of social consciousness of later years. What started as a pleasant summer morning has ended with time's annihilating power. "Ah, no; the years O! / And the rotten rose is ript from the wall."

The fourth and final stanza takes place in autumn and records the Gifford family's move to their "high new house" of "Bedford

Terrace." Frequent mention of bad weather is made in *Some Recollections*, suggesting the rain here, though the "[c]locks and carpets and chairs / On the lawn all day" is Hardy's imaginative rendition of the actual move to their new home in Bodmin. Hardy did not visit Plymouth until after Emma's death when he went to visit some of her relatives. With all their "brightest things" on display for all to see, this last stanza ends with the cruelest suggestion yet—namely, that even the memory of the family cannot escape the ravages of time. As the rain "ploughs" down upon their engraved names, any record of the family's existence is itself threatened with absolute extinction with the passage of time. What was once a gentle and life-sustaining drop of rain has been transformed into a cruel instrument of Nature destroying that which it previously nurtured. "Ah, no; the years, the years; / Down their carved names the rain-drop ploughs."

"During Wind and Rain"

SAMUEL HYNES ON THE IMAGERY OF TONE

[Samuel Hynes is the author of *The Edwardian Turn of Mind* (1968); *A War Imagined: The First World War and English Culture* (1991); and *The Growing Seasons: An American Boyhood Before the War* (2003). In the following excerpt, Hynes discusses imagery of tone in "During Wind and Rain."]

"During Wind and Rain" illustrates two points about Hardy's imagery—it is homogeneous and self-contained, and it is highly selective. Hardy's images, without notable exception, are native to the world which we call Wessex. This does not, of course, make the poems "Wessex poems" in the sense that Hardy's best novels are "Wessex novels"; that is, the poems neither create nor depend on a sense of locale. By selecting the "features that matter," Hardy keeps the focus of the poem on the emotional weighting rather than on the image itself.

Individual images are not often striking; they derive their effectiveness more from the accretions of emotion which tradition has given to certain experiences than from pictorial vividness or the impact of oddness. The scenes are rarely realized in any great detail, and few readers, I should think, actually visualize the rain and the darkness: archetypal imagery bypasses this step to comprehension. The emotion-producing detail is there—the falling leaf or the night wind—but the specific surroundings are largely ignored. The imagery produces tone rather than picture; it is, in the words of Turner that Hardy quotes: "something else which shall have upon the spectator an approximative erect to that of the real." Images may, on occasion, be sharp and clear—Hardy had an eye for the small, significant detail—but the background is seldom filled in, so that pictorially the images are incomplete, like a painter's rough cartoons. They are not, of course, any less effective for their bareness.

This imagistic bareness, this unwillingness to indulge the

sensual for its own sake, is simply another aspect of the restraint and decorum which characterized Hardy's entire life. Mrs. Hardy tells us that he could not stand to be touched, and, one senses this fastidious withdrawal from direct physical contact with life in much of the poetry. For example, he rarely used images involving the "contact" senses of touch and taste, or the kinesthetic sense, preferring images of sight and sound—the senses which can operate at a distance. Through such devices he made his poems those of an observer rather than of an agent; his speaker is consistently *outside* the event, observing it but not involved in it. "Afterwards," one of the most imagistic (and one of the loveliest) of Hardy's poems, demonstrates this point very well:

> When the Present has latched its postern behind my tremulous stay,
>   And the May month flaps its glad green leaves like wings,
> Delicate-filmed as new-spun silk, will the neighbours say,
>   "He was a man who used to notice such things"?
>
> If it be in the dusk when, like an eyelid's soundless blink,
>   The dewfall-hawk comes crossing the shades to alight
> Upon the wind-warped upland thorn, a gazer may think,
>   "To him this must have been a familiar sight"
>
> If I pass during some nocturnal blackness, mothy and warm,
>   When the hedgehog travels furtively over the lawn,
> One may say, "He strove that such, innocent creatures should
>   come to no harm,
>   But he could do little for them; and now he is gone."
>
> If, when hearing that I have been stilled at last, they stand at
>   the door,
>   Watching the full-starred heavens that winter sees,
> Will this thought rise on those who will meet my face no more,
>   "He was one who had an eye for such mysteries"?
>
> And will any say when my bell of quittance is heard in the gloom,
>   And a crossing breeze cuts a pause in its outrollings,
> Till they rise again, as they were a new bell's boom,
>   "He hears it not now, but used to notice such things"?
>
>   (*Collected Poems, p.* 521)

The speaker in this poem is very like Hardy as I have been describing him—a man who "notices" from a distance, who has "an eye for much mysteries," who is familiar with the sights and sounds of his rural world. The principal images in the poem are, very characteristically, observed from a distance: the hawk on the thorn, the hedgehog on the lawn, the stars, the distant bell. Of these the speaker is a sensitive and precise observer; he knows the texture of new leaves and the way hawks and hedgehogs move. But though he "notices such things," he can do little for them: there is no interaction between observer and observed.

—Samuel Hynes. *The Pattern of Hardy's Poetry*. Chapel Hill, N.C.: The University of North Carolina Press (1961): 123–26.

GEOFFREY HARVEY ON THE UNIVERSALITY OF LIVED EXPERIENCE

[Geoffrey Harvey is the author of *The Complete Critical Guide to Thomas Hardy* (2003) and "Thomas Hardy's Poetry of Transcendence" (1978). In the following excerpt, Harvey discusses the way in which the lived experience is given universal validity in "During Wind and Rain."]

In Hardy's poetry such moments are won by the mind itself, for only the mind can give meaning to reality. Hardy's moments of vision are created out of lived experience, and their fundamental commitment to life gives them a universal validity. This wholeness of life, mind and art is perhaps best seen in what is probably his greatest poem, and the final one that I wish to consider here, 'During Wind and Rain', in which Hardy draws once more on his memories of Emma, this time of her family home in Devon:[17]

> They sing their dearest songs—
> He, she, all of them—yea,
> Treble and tenor and bass,
>   And one to play;
> With the candles mooning each face....

Ah, no; the years O!
How the sick leaves reel down in throngs!

They clear the creeping moss—
Elders and juniors—aye,
Making the pathways neat
    And the garden gay;
And they build a shady seat....
    Ah, no; the years, the years;
See, the white storm-birds wing across!

They are blithely breakfasting all—
Men and maidens—yea,
Under the summer tree,
    With a glimpse of the bay,
While pet fowl come to the knee....
    Ah, no; the years O!
And the rotten rose is ript from the wall.

They change to a high new house,
He, she, all of them—aye,
Clocks and carpets and chairs
    On the lawn all day,
And brightest things that are theirs....
    Ah, no; the years, the years;
Down their carved names the rain-drop ploughs.

In some respects this is a puzzling poem and critics have responded to it in various ways. Basically the poem is divided into four discrete, beautiful moments of vision which embrace human fellowship and harmony as positive joys, each of which, however, is undercut by a remorseless refrain, which reminds the reader of the inevitable passing of time, and of mortality. A straightforward approach to the poem's meaning is to regard this division as marking a simple structural irony of the kind which operates in *Satires of Circumstance*. The vision of domestic harmony on a winter evening in the first stanza, with its magical co-operation between fact and imagination, is contrasted with the falling leaves. In the second stanza the family's instinct to combat the burgeoning of the natural world in the spring, by clearing the moss in order to make way for human concerns, is contrasted with the threatening spring gales and the malevolent storm birds. The domestication of nature is significant in the third stanza as the context for human fellowship, imaged by the sacramental breakfast under the summer tree; it too, however, finds its destroyer in time, which rips the 'rotten rose' from the wall. In the final stanza the family's removal to a new house, symbolising their courageous attempt to redefine their humanity in different places, puts their achievement of a poised, assured selfhood in jeopardy, like, their furniture on the lawn exposed to the weather. Time, present in the rhythm of the seasons, co-operates with place and with human lives, yet it also carries a threat, a reminder of the inherent futility of even their noblest actions.

One view of the poem is that Hardy simply offers two distinct perspectives and allows them to stand in silent commentary on each other. Another interpretation regards these moments of vision, incomplete as they are, as having greater vividness, more impact and significance than the negative images of the refrains. But a clue to a more fruitful approach to the meaning of 'During Wind and Rain' is given by its title, which is an echo of Feste's song that concludes *Twelfth Night*, a song which is itself both a profound recognition of the fundamental absurdity of the universe and a beautiful celebration of human life and values. Hardy's poem achieves a similar transcendence. In 'During Wind and Rain' the moments of vision are not created in opposition to, or even in ignorance of, the waste and futility of life; nor are those poles of human experience permitted to stand in mute dichotomy; rather the terror of a meaningless universe is incorporated into the poem, not simply as a structural unity, but into each discrete moment of vision, subtly qualifying it and becoming part of its statement. This becomes evident if one pays close attention to Hardy's superb technique. His breaking-up of the elaborate symmetry of the four stanzas by his metrical variations in the last line of each suggests how, for the neutral observer, each idyllic moment is dissolved by a harsher reality. Yet the cluster of images conveying the delicate world of the poem also contains within it this ineluctable force of dissolution. The beautiful image in the opening stanza of the candles 'mooning each face', both factual and visionary, includes within it the suggestion of decay, for even as they illumine the gathering the candles are burning out, and the moon itself is a powerful traditional symbol of change. Similarly, the springtime vision of the second stanza comprehends the creeping moss, which remains an enduring threat to human significance; while in the third stanza the sea, which can be glimpsed by the breakfasting group, is also a potent symbol of the mutability of life and experience. And, finally, the furniture left in the open air on the lawn makes a poignant image of human vulnerability and frailty. The moments of vision themselves thus include a strong sense of an indifferent universe, of dissolution as inevitable and of human action as ultimately absurd. But this knowledge, which permeates the places in which they choose to act, is shared by the inhabitants of the world of the poem. The careful symmetry of these stanzas is the formal correlative of the way in which they nevertheless impose order and beauty on the flux of experience. Their awareness of a terrifying nullity at the heart of things is transcended by actions which celebrate love, fellowship and the sheer joy of being, which display a powerful sense of achieved selfhood, of purpose, adventure and gaiety.

NOTE

17. See *Some Recollections by Emma Hardy*, ed. Evelyn Hardy and Robert Gittings (London, 1961) p. 5.

> —Geoffrey Harvey. *The Romantic Tradition in Modern English Poetry: Rhetoric and Experience*. New York: St. Martin's Press (1986): 66–69.

JOANNA CULLEN BROWN ON JOURNEY THROUGH THE STAGES OF LIFE

[Joanna Cullen Brown is the editor of *Figures in a Wessex Landscape: Thomas Hardy's Picture of English Country Life* (1987) and *Let Me Enjoy the Earth: Thomas Hardy and Nature* (1990). In the following excerpt from her book, Brown discusses "During Wind and Rain" as Hardy's journey through the significant stages of life.]

It is during a quickening storm of wind and rain that Hardy looks back on the journey through life, the stages of the storm matching the more significant stages of life. At first only the rising wind makes itself known as, in contrast to the harmonious scene within, images of universal decay and finality swirl down in the sick leaves—"reeling" suggesting a variety of images from drunken or beaten helplessness to its opposite in a ghastly *danse macabre*. Then, like the emergent slug which warned Gabriel Oak of impending rain, other creatures take note of the portents, and the birds (explicitly white, not only because they are probably seabirds, but presumably also because white is often a sinister colour for Hardy) seeking shelter herald the hiss and lash of the destroying storm. The poem is tightly and carefully structured, the image in each stanza's last line connecting closely to that of the next stanza—as the storm birds lead to the fowls, the wall to the high new house. The reader is swung, in Hardy's most typical counterpoint, between contrasting themes: between memory and the intrusive present setting, the pictures deriving from the past and the single, final lines depicting the storm in the present; between candlelight and shadow, the harmony, happiness and brightness of the actors, and the heavy threat of the storm; between their busy occupations and the repeated interruptions and obstruction of "the years, the years," which, in token of this, alone of all lines do not rhyme with any other. This ballad-like refrain emphasises the theme of the lifetime passing. It checks us with "Ah, no;". It separates human life from the forces of Nature; and points to the storm which, in its destructiveness, its denial of all the past life images, becomes, particularly in the poem's final line, a concrete expression of Time—much as do the rain and darkness of "At Castle Boterel".

The final line indeed comes as something of a shock,[12] when the scene of the objects standing up on the lawn blends, as in a film, into the gravestone standing in the green of the churchyard. As the last lines of the other stanzas are often difficult to say, thick with consonants or alliteration, so is it particularly here: it enforces our attention with almost every word in the line heavily stressed, imitating the fundamental human labour of carving and ploughing.

The image of the plough is rich in underlying meanings. It can be linked with the earlier activity of clearing the creeping moss, which Thom Gunn likens to the burning of couch-grass, "a quiet clearing of space in nature so as to make room for human assertions."[13] But one can also think of clichés like "whole civilisations disappearing under the plough". It is a destructive and obliterating instrument which can reduce everything in its path to dust. Nature, with its rain that falls upon the just and the unjust, obliterates our own, personal, human patterns, as it has been doing in its interventions against our memories throughout the poem. (For the first time, in this line the image representing the Present now also includes the family, hitherto always kept safely in the Past.) It is another of Hardy's favourite contrasts and incongruities that he should make a gentle raindrop "plough" (…)

In the final line of "During Wind and Rain" Hardy finds that what he has been drawing in the poem—a lifetime of memories, but described in the present as if they were still being lived—turns out to be drawn in dead names on a gravestone. The memories, the life, seem fresh and bright; but they end up superseded, merely a bare outline, a skeleton where once was flesh and blood; and an outline that is steadily eroded by the continuing rain. With his usual care for structure Hardy sees to it that the light downward reel of leaves at the beginning is matched by the stressed, implacable downward pitch of obliterating water at the end.

The power of this poem can be felt even though—or perhaps because—so much is left to the imagination. Hardy says nothing about who these people are—"he, she, all of them"—nor why he picks out certain of their activities, nor why, for example, their clocks and chairs should be out all day. He often deliberately writes his poem around a gap; and this invitation to participate, to make them work, gives readers part of their satisfaction in his poetry. It has much in common with the ballad tradition which is so important a background to his poems: here are the same mysteries, the same vivid depiction of only partially explained human actions. Like a ballad, this poem universalises and generalises human experience. We do not know who the speaker is, but he seems to speak for us as he reflects on the stages of human life and its setting within the world and time.

I was quick to bloom; late to ripen.

It is arguable whether any other English poet has ripened so fruitfully, or so finely nourished his poetry with the wisdom and experience of great age.[17]

NOTES

12. Which Taylor compares with the shock of the eerie light change at the end of *The Wind's Prophecy.*

13. Thom Gunn, *op cit, Casebook* 223

17. W.B. Yeats, whose greatest period was probably the last twenty years of his life, is the obvious comparison.

> —Joanna Cullen Brown. *A Journey Into Thomas Hardy's Poetry.* London: W.H. Allen & Co Plc (1989): 175–78.

U.C. KNOEPFLMACHER ON AUTOBIOGRAPHICAL DETAILS

[U.C. Knoepflmacher is the author of *Ventures into Childland: Victorians, Fairy Tales, and Femininity* (1998); *Religious Humanism and the Victorian Novel* (1965) and co-editor of *The Endurance of Frankenstein: Essays on Mary Shelley's Novel* (1979). In the excerpt below from his article, "Hardy Ruins: Female Spaces and Male Designs" Knoepflmacher discusses the autobiographical details of "During Wind and Rain."]

The houses depicted in nineteenth-century British poetry differ substantially from earlier representations of a patriarchal seat in poems such as Marvell's "Upon Appleton House" and Pope's "Epistle to Burlington" as well as from the male mansions domesticated by female inhabitants in nineteenth-century realistic novels. In a century that separated an inner circle of female domesticity from an outer sphere of male traffic, the home became increasingly feminized, associated with childhood and hence with nurturance.[1] Yet a good many imaginative writers responded to this division by attempting to integrate gender opposites within a culturally defined feminine space. In *Jane Eyre*, for example, Ferndean replaces Thornfield Hall as a site in which an independent heroine can animate the paralyzed Rochester and enter a more equitable union. This integration, however, does not work in the same way for poets as it does for novelists; likewise, it works differently for men and women.[2] For Thomas Hardy, who preferred poetry to fiction, the recovery of the feminine was the propelling force behind his finest lyrics. Over his poetic career, Hardy wavered in his faith that the feminine, which he associated with the houses of childhood, could be recovered without the compromise of adult masculinity. Eventually, in his old age, he nonetheless managed to effect the "return to the native land" that Freud identified as a maternal "home" (Cixous and Clément 93).

The structures of desire devised by Hardy's nineteenth-century poetic predecessors dramatize the difficulty of finding a feminine space capable of annulling gender and rendering sexual difference immaterial. By way of contrast, the patriarchal houses that novelists enlist as transformational spaces allow female occupants room enough to break down too rigidly gendered opposites. Just as Pemberley Hall crowns Elizabeth Bennet's efforts to soften Darcy's male pride (while simultaneously acting as a patriarchal corrective to her own prejudices), so are male mansions renovated when entered by Jane Eyre, Catherine Linton, Helen Huntingdon, Esther Summerson, and even Hardy's Bathsheba Everdene.[3] In Romantic and Victorian poetry, however, such a process of renewal and restabilizing remains far more problematic. Ruins, rather than living buildings, predominate in works in which a woman's abode, rather than a man's, becomes directly or indirectly associated with what Bachelard sees as a "dream-memory" of an original maternal envelope (15). (...)

"During Wind and Rain" conflates details scattered over many pages in *Some Recollections*. Drawing on the description of

Bedford Terrace, the "pleasant home" that proved to be his wife's last secure haven, Thomas relies on the hindsight by which Emma regarded this building as full of "curious omens" betokening death and dispersal for a family soon to fall from "so high" an eminence (*Some Recollections* 30–32).[13] The "They" of the poem are deliberately left unidentified. Blended through their music, the members of this domestic group lack individuality:

> They sing their dearest songs—
> He, she, all of them—yea,
> Treble and tenor and bass,
>   And one to play,
> With the candles mooning each face....
>   Ah, no; the years O!
> How the sick leaves reel down in throngs!   (1–7)

Who *are* "he" and "she"? The lack of specificity allows the speaker, who is acutely aware of severance, to insert his own presence among the singers. The "nameless" singing opens an "elsewhere" for a man "capable of becoming a woman" (Cixous and Clément 93, 98). Stranded in a different era by the passage of many years, he nonetheless can insinuate himself into this alien, vanished household and regard it as if he were there. Despite its insistence on separation and change, "During Wind and Rain" thus reconstitutes a "he" and a "she" among "all of them." Through a time warp, ruin and wholeness are simultaneously perceived; dispersion and integration can somehow coexist:

> They change to a high new house,
> He, she, all of them—aye,
> Clocks, and carpets and chairs
>   On the lawn all day,
> And brightest things that are theirs....
>   Ah, no; the years, the years;
> Down their carved names the rain-drop ploughs. (22–28)

The scattered material objects on the lawn—with the clocks

taking an ominous precedence in the list of a household's "brightest things"—will become permanently dissipated when a single day is replaced by "the years." Yet, as the last line shocks us into recognizing, the animated occupants of the building have long ago become inert objects themselves, reduced into names on tombstones. Only the single raindrop, so like the tear of a single mourner, can restore movement, stirring and plowing up lives that have crumbled into clay.

In combining his sense of abandonment by his wife with her recorded pangs of separation from Bedford Terrace, Hardy makes the "he" and "she" of the poem stand for more than the parents whom Emma Lavinia Gifford was forced to leave behind. They also represent the aged poet and the young "she" he imaginatively joins by adding his own lyric to the song that had once united "all of them." But his vicarious entry into another's family romance suggests that he is processing a much earlier separation. Long before Emma's death, Thomas had fashioned a powerful poem associating the interior of a house with an ecstatic self-annulment through music.

NOTES

1. The two most famous Victorian representations of the feminine domestic ideal are Coventry Patmore's *Angel in the House* (1854–62) and John Ruskin's "Of Queens' Gardens" (1865). Earlier writers such as Sarah Ellis and Sarah Lewis, however, had already upheld the privatization of domestic space. The ambiguities and contradictions of sexual difference marking out separate spheres in this period have been amply analyzed by contemporary critics; see, for example, Armstrong, Auerbach, Christ, Davidoff and Hall, Gilbert and Gubar, Houghton, Poovey, and Welsh.

2. The great difficulty faced by a female child in establishing ego boundaries in a patriarchal culture allows some feminists to argue that a girl's relation to the unconscious, the body, and maternal rhythms is closer than a boy's (see Chodorow). While differing in their fundamental philosophical and political programs, French feminist critics such as Hélène Cixous, Catherine Clément, and Julia Kristeva nonetheless posit that poets, female or male, are "complex, mobile, open" in allowing the opposite sex "entrance" into them (Cixous and Clément 84–85). Kristeva, without relying on a theory of feminine language, demonstrates how male writers, predominantly modernist poets like Mallarmé and Baudelaire, allow the semiotic "chora," linked to the mother's body, to speak through their writing (93–98). Poetry, closer to song and pure rhythm, she argues, is less controlled than prose by the symbolic strictures of syntax.

3. Still, Gothic enclosures are far more unstable than the houses found in the

traditional novel of manners. Decaying (like Wildfell Hall) or razed (like Thornfield), such buildings display a "'ruined' architecture" that cannot be mended (Gordon 231). Thus, Hareton and the second Catherine must forsake the Heights for the Grange, while Esther Summerson must found a second Bleak House, For the transgressive qualities of the Gothic, see Jackson, Sedgwick, and Wilt, among others.

13. As Evelyn Hardy and Robert Gittings were the first to recognize, Hardy not only drew on these and other details in his wife's descriptions but also chose to stress the downpour she regarded as an emblem of her final separation from her Plymouth childhood: "never did so watery an omen portend such dullnesses, and sadnesses and sorrows as this did for us" (E. Hardy 37, 68).

—U.C. Knoepflmacher. *PMLA* vol. 105, no. 5 (October 1990): 1055–56 and 1063–64.

JOHN PAUL RIQUELME ON THE INFLUENCE OF SHELLEY

[John Paul Riquelme is the author of *Teller and Tale in Joyce's Fiction: Oscillating Perspectives* (1983) and *Harmony of Dissonances: T.S. Eliot, Romanticism and Imagination* (1991), and the editor of *Tess of the D'Urbervilles* (1998). In the excerpt below from his article, "The modernity of Thomas Hardy's poetry" Riquelme compares "During Wind and Rain" to Shelley's "Ode to the West Wind."]

The radically ambiguous effects, refusal of consolation, and negativity persist in ways that respond to Romantic poets besides Wordsworth. "During Wind and Rain," published in *Moments of Vision and Miscellaneous Verses (1917)*, owes a clear debt to Shelley's "Ode to the West Wind." Harold Bloom even calls Hardy's poem "a grandchild" of Shelley's.[3] In saying that, however, Bloom claims not just that wind, rain, leaves, and storm are important in both poems but that Hardy is a late-Romantic poet who follows Shelley thematically and not just chronologically. That is not the case. Shelley's poem is formally elegant, with long lines of verse arranged into five numbered parts that combine the Shakespearean sonnet with an English version of terza rima in imitation of Dante. Hardy's poem is a ballad, a popular form as far from Dante and Shakespearean sonnets as Hardy is from Shelley. The difference is apparent in the poems' contrasting diction. In Shelley, "the leaves dead / Are driven like ghosts from an enchanter fleeing." In Hardy, "the sick leaves reel down in throngs!" (*CPW*, II, p. 239). "Reel" suggests going round in a whirling motion, but, in the context of singing and the playing of music referred to earlier in the same stanza, "reel" can also call to mind the Scottish dance. In this poem, which concerns change and death, the dance is a *danse macabre* or dance of death in which all participate. Shelley's poem projects instead a cyclical process that renews life, as the closing optimistically asserts: "O Wind, / If Winter comes, can Spring be far behind?"

Shelley's closing apostrophe to the wind differs from Hardy's use of apostrophe. Both apostrophe and personification can suggest that a human speaker and humanized nature are mutually supportive. Hardy regularly avoids that suggestion. Shelley's poem begins and ends with an apostrophic invocation to the wind, addressed as "O wild West Wind" in the first line. Several times in the poem, at the end of a line Shelley's speaker invokes the wind as "O thou" or enjoins it to listen with "oh, hear!" Hardy mimics but transforms Shelley's use of apostrophe at line-ends in two of his stanzas by closing the ballad-like refrain at the sixth line with the "O" of an apparent apostrophe: "the years O!" (lines 6, 20). But this "O" is the sound of the voice sighing, a sign of loss rather than an indication of full-throated lyric address. Hardy does not begin and end his poem in a Shelleyan way with apostrophes to an aspect of nature that appears to stand for the imagination. Instead, he literalizes the wind by making it part of the natural context in which the poem's events and his presentation of those events occur. T.S. Eliot does something similar in "Rhapsody on a Windy Night," published in *Prufrock and Other Observations* (1917) the same year as *Moments of Vision*.

This literalizing of Romantic figures, like the use of *cow* in "Nature's Questioning," creates a revisionary distance between the later poem and the earlier Romantic one. Hardy's "O" at the end of a line rhymes internally with "Ah, no" from earlier in the line and expresses a response to "the years." That is, instead of addressing "the years" as human by saying "O Years," Hardy links "O" internally with "no" and with time's passage. In the alternative versions of the refrain, "the years O" becomes "the years, the years" (lines 13, 27) in a repetition that explains what "O" means. Rather than inspiring a prophetic response, which Shelley requests of the wind, the years, along with the wind and the rain, define the context, time, and the weather, in which life proceeds to its inevitable end.

At the end of Shelley's poem, the speaker asks that the wind carry a trumpeting prophecy through his lips to an "unawakened earth," presumably in order to wake it up. The west wind and the poet's breath would fuse in poetic singing. In this projected mutuality of voice, Shelley has sung to and for the wind, which he asks now to sing through him. There is singing in "During Wind and Rain," at the beginning, but it is singing by "He, she, all of them" (line 2), apparently real people in a domestic scene, not by a poet intent on prophecy. The domestication of song works in tandem with the literalizing of wind. At the end of Hardy's poem, instead of the promise of prophetic song, we hear that "Down their carved names the rain-drop ploughs" (line 28). The scene has become a cemetery in the rain, with drops running down the names of those who once sang. The rain has become a tear that responds to the fact that those who lie in the earth cannot be awakened.

The tear of rain indicates more than lamentation about a loss, for it is figuratively engaged in the agricultural work of ploughing, which is related to carving as an act of marking a surface through human labor. Unlike Shelley, Hardy focuses in his poem's ending not on imaginative wind and prophetic singing but on the human labor of carving, ploughing, and, by extension, writing as work that remembers what once was but has now passed. The response to Shelley involves centrally a corrective gesture in which the "O" of apostrophe is negated, opposed, and written over by the "Ah, no" repeated in all four stanzas in the lines of refrain. Instead of emphasizing a wind that is always there to inspire poetic singing, Hardy stresses time's passage and the changes that compose human history. Rather than imitating the Romantic precursors to whom he responds, Hardy expresses distinctive attitudes. The poetic future that "During Wind and Rain" anticipates and enables includes Seamus Heaney's

"Digging," in which the poet chooses to dig with his pen. For Heaney, as for Hardy, writing resembles working with the earth or with stone, not Shelley's prophetic, wind-inspired trumpeting.

NOTE

3. Harold Bloom, *A Map of Misreading* (New York: Oxford University Press, 1975), p. 21.

> —John Paul Riquelme. *The Cambridge Companion to Thomas Hardy*, ed. Dale Kramer. Cambridge and New York: Cambridge University Press (1999): 208–10.

JOHN HUGHES ON MUSIC AS A LINK TO THE TRANSCENDENT

[John Hughes is the author of *Lines of Flight: Reading Deleuze with Hardy, Gissing, Conrad, Woolf* (1997). In the following excerpt, Hughes discusses "During Wind and Rain" as a visionary poem in which music is provides a link to the transcendent. From *'Ecstatic Sound': Music and Individuality in the Work of Thomas Hardy*.]

At first glance, 'During Wind and Rain' is another poem which uses music to capture the complexities of a present moment that in the poet's mind has its final meaning in relation to the future whose past it will be. The final line in each stanza extracts from its scene of collective blitheness a portent of transience:

> They sing their dearest songs—
> He, she, all of them—
> Treble and tenor and bass,
>   And one to play;
> With candles mooning each face....
>   Ah, no; the years O!
> How the sick leaves reel down in throngs!
>   ('During Wind and Rain', *Complete Poems*, p. 495)

Nevertheless, more than this, as Lucas puts it, 'During Wind and

Rain' is a 'truly visionary poem', one in which the present opens onto the eternal, as well as onto the past and the future. The poem, he writes, catches in its scenes a genuinely 'timeless vision balanced', though it is, 'against the steady progress of time' (*Modern English Poetry*, p. 47). This section pursues this capacity of music to signal to the 'timeless' in Lucas's phrase, beyond its capacity to introduce into a scene the signs of the past and of the future.

Once again, as the lines quoted make clear, we can link music to what is affirmed as transcendent in the transient present, to those 'timeless' values, in Lucas's phrase, of individual expression and relatedness that Hardy always associates with it. In a general way, the ontological complexities of music itself account in part for its capacity to participate in these temporal shifts and interpolations. As an art of duration, in the first place, it ties together sensation and memory. In the second place, even in the most mundane description, music is also an art of the 'timeless', since it retains an ideality, a power of self-differentiation, outside the logic of the calendar: a musical work necessarily transcends the successive circumstances in which it is variably instantiated and interpreted.

In this latter respect, one can describe how music reawakens in the hearer a sense of spiritual possibility that can, for a short time, alleviate alienation. Beyond its own intrinsic pleasures, as we have seen, the transcendent effects of music make it possible to relive remembered joys. However, in personal terms, what often appears most important and valuable is not simply that musical experiences bring back the past, but that they revive in the older poet enduring values of selfhood more fully expressed in the affective readiness, pliancy and intensity of youth.[13]

NOTE

13. John Lucas, 'Hardy Among the Poets', *Critical Survey*, Vol. 5, no. 2 (Oxford: Oxford University Press, 1993), p. 201.

—John Hughes. *'Ecstatic Sound': Music and Individuality in the Work of Thomas Hardy*. Burlington, Vermont: Ashgate Publishing Company (2001): 174–75.

"The Convergence of the Twain"

Completed on April 24, 1912, "Convergence of the Twain," was one of eighteen lyrics that comprised Hardy's "Poems of 1912–13," and was later placed in the volume entitled *Satires of Circumstances*. However, this poem first appeared in the program of the "Dramatic and Operatic Matinée in Aid of the 'Titanic' Disaster Fund," given at Covent Garden Theatre on May 14. The poem concerns the sinking of the White Star Liner *Titanic* on April 15, 1912 on her maiden voyage in which 1,513 passengers perished from a total of 2,224 on board. The ship sank at 2:20 a.m., less than three hours after it smashed into an iceberg at full speed. The passengers on board included many of great wealth and fame and those in high positions. Among the passengers who perished was an acquaintance of Hardy, Mr. William T. Stead, editor of the *Review of Reviews* who, in 1899, had asked Hardy to express his opinion on 'A Crusade of Peace' in a periodical he was about to publish under the name of *War Against War*. Touted for being an unsinkable ship, the neglect in providing a sufficient number of lifeboats lead to a staggering death toll. These facts all play a significant role in Hardy's poem. Its passenger list could boast of the most prominent of New York society while the ship itself contained such lavish furnishings and amenities as Turkish Baths, an elaborate gymnasium, a palm court "with real ivory and crimson ramblers," mahogany panelling, bandstands and organs, and immense stores of wines, cream, and foods of all kinds. Along with its numerous indulgences, both passengers and crew believed it was invincible against the elements. "That attitude, reflecting the hubris of an over-complacent world soon to be plunged into a war of unprecedented savagery, was a perfect subject for Tom, who did not look in a sanguine spirit upon the notion of 'human progress' and deplored those who so foolishly did." (Seymour-Smith). Thus, the tone of the poem is more illustrative of the devastation brought about by human excesses than mournful for the tragedy that ensued.

Within the context of an international tragedy, "The Convergence of the Twain," a poetic narration of the ill-fated destiny of the *Titanic* becomes the impetus for a universal allegory of the fate that awaits those who place their value in material objects. The tragic end to which the passengers came, both rich and poor, was the result of both the ship's owners and its wealthy patrons being seduced into believing such a lavishly appointed luxury ship to be invulnerable to the perils of the sea. Furthermore, in Hardy's narration of the massive death and destruction, it is also significant that the *Titanic* was on its maiden voyage, a fact that becomes important in the second half of the poem. It is also interesting to note that in his description of the proud ship, a symbol of vain-gloriousness, there is no mention of the loss of human life. Rather, it is the *Titanic* itself that is somewhat humanized and represented as the victim of the Immanent Will's rebuke. In this poem, there is a depersonalization of a national tragedy from the very outset. Finally, Hardy uses a feminine description and rhetoric for the *Titanic* throughout the poem as the focus of the poem shifts from the sinking of the great ship to a symbolic description of a passionate sexual encounter between the *Titanic* and the iceberg. Hence, the title "The Convergence of the Twain."

The poem contains two distinct thematic divisions of five stanzas each. Each of the first five stanzas provide vivid images of the depths to which all the *Titanic*'s prized possessions have sunk. From the very outset, we are given a detailed description of the death of a beautiful and vain woman whose misguided values have plummeted to the very bottom of the ocean floor. "Deep from human vanity, / And the Pride of Life that planned her, stilly couches she." Yet for all her feminine characteristics, the *Titanic* is also depicted as yet another aspect of the failure inherent in a mechanical universe as described in the analysis of "Hap," a world devoid of hope, redemption, or transcendent potential. And in his description of the buried ship, there is also an element of irony. "Steel chambers, late the pyres / Of her salamandrine fires, / Cold currents thrid, and turn to rhythmic tidal lyres." According to mythic tradition, the salamander was believed to be able to live in and withstand fire, yet the *Titanic*, a myth in its own right, was utterly unable to do so. Thus, as a *momento mori*, we are given a vivid description of the erosion and invasion of grotesque sea life that invade its once stately domain. "Over the mirrors meant / to glass the opulent / The sea worm crawls—grotesque, slimed, dumb, indifferent." By the fifth stanza, in a dark subterranean world, "dim moon-eyed fishes" swim with the biblical caveat that all is vanity. "What does this vaingloriousness down here?"

In the sixth stanza, the allegory continues with a statement that a higher power, a force aligned with nature, controls men's destinies, "The Immanent Will that stirs and urges everything," yet the focus shifts to the fashioning of an ugly male counterpart, a terrifying entity, "a sinister mate" that is purposely intended to bring the *Titanic* to ruin. "For her—so gaily great—/ A Shape of Ice, for the time fat and dissociate." And, the most frightening aspect of all is that their union is absolute and unavoidable. As the beautifully adorned ship approaches, growing "In stature, grace, and hue," the two mates are utterly alone and abandoned with no hope of rescue. "Alien they seemed to be: / No mortal eye could see / The intimate welding of their later history." And, thus, the moment of their sexual union is also the moment of their demise. "Till the Spinner of the Years / Said 'Now!' And each one hears, /And consummation comes, and jars two hemispheres." The beautiful and vain-glorious ship, enticing to all those that had admired her, ornamented as if for marriage and on her way to meet her bridegroom, has now become the victim of her own blind vanity.

"The Convergence of the Twain"

SAMUEL HYNES ON ELEMENTS OF CONTRADICTION

[Samuel Hynes is the author of *The Edwardian Turn of Mind* (1968); *A War Imagined: The First World War and English Culture* (1991); and *The Growing Seasons: An American Boyhood Before the War* (2003). In the following excerpt, Hynes discusses elements of contradiction in "The Convergence of the Twain."]

Briefly, Hardy's antinomial pattern works this way: thesis (usually a circumstance commonly accepted as good—marriage, youth, young love, the reunion of husband and wife) is set against antithesis (infidelity, age, death, separation) to form an ironic complex, which is left unresolved. One might, generally speaking, say that the pattern is built on the relation of appearance and reality. In many of the poems this is true on a very simple level, as in "A Wife in London" or "Architectural Masks," which contrasts the exteriors of two houses with their occupants. But in more complicated poems the generalization is only valid if we recognize that appearance has its own kind of subjective truth—deluded love is still love—and is not merely an illusion to be destroyed; or to put it another way, reality is not morally superior to appearance, though it is always more powerful and always destructive.

It is in terms of this appearance–reality relationship that the inconsistencies of Hardy's philosophy are most apparent—in his poetry he could not be true to his pessimistic vision. Words like "lovingkindness" and "life-loyalties" creep in in spite of the philosophy, and the darkling thrush sings of "some blessed Hope, whereof he knew / And I was unaware." Perhaps no poet could be consistently ateleologically deterministic and remain a poet; for Hardy, at any rate, it is this antinomial tension between his thought and, his feelings that gives his verse its characteristic pattern and its integrity, and which gives order, though a minimal order, to the chaos of experience.

The antinomial structure is most apparent in Hardy's most obviously ironic poems, like the "Satires of Circumstance" (Hardy used satire and irony interchangeably), but the better poems also have it, and draw from it a complexity which the weaker do not have. On the most obvious level, Hardy's antinomial set of mind is evident in his habit of dividing his poems into two parts: in the first part one term is set up, in the second its opposite is set against it, and their mutual antagonisms are ironically, but dispassionately remarked. Often Hardy made the pattern more obvious by using a two-stanza form; or two numbered sections, each devoted to one term of the antinomy, as in "A Merrymaking in Question," "Before and After Summer," "The Coquette and After"; the titles of the last two are further indications of the two-part structure, as well as of the role time plays in it.

This characteristic structure can be demonstrated in virtually any one of Hardy's nine-hundred-odd poems; I will take as a single example one of his commonest anthology pieces, "The Convergence of the Twain." (…)

Here the thesis is obviously the "smart ship," the antithesis the iceberg. The poem divides into two equal parts at stanza VI, the first part establishing the qualities of the thesis-term, the second introducing the antithesis. This is the most obvious antinomial pattern in the poem, but there are also a number of ancillary ones. The diction, for example, is of two distinct kinds: the lush, exotic, polysyllabic language of the first part works against the monosyllables of the second. The first part is heavy with modifiers, with active verbs, with particular, physical substantives; the second is bare and abstract by comparison. Virtually all of the poem's imagery is concentrated in the description of the ship; the iceberg is simply a "Shape of Ice" growing "in shadowy silent distance."

The final stanza brings the two complex terms of the antinomy—by now they are ship-world and iceberg-world—together, but the meeting is not a synthesizing one; it "jars two hemispheres," but it does not answer the question that the "moon-eyed fishes" asked in stanza V: "What does this vaingloriousness down here?" The iceberg is the efficient cause of the ship sinking, but for Hardy there is no final cause, and the answer is only a recognition that there are no answers.

The "Convergence" is an example of the discovery in a public event of a situation which Hardy more often saw in personal, human terms—the disastrous accident which shouldn't have happened but did, "the ill-judged execution of the well-judged plan of things." He made the similarity to his more personal situations more striking by setting the convergence in terms of sexual union: *couches, ravish, mate, consummation* make of the collision a kind or cosmic mismarriage (marriage in Hardy is almost invariably a paradigm of his antinomial vision of the world, a symbol of the destructive interaction of opposites).

In spite of the presence of the Immanent Will there is no philosophy in the "Convergence"; there is only Hardy's sense of the inscrutable universal irony of things. It is a good poem, good because it is ironic and not philosophical, for Hardy's home-made philosophy usually betrayed him in his verse, while his ironic sense was his greatest poetic asset. Irony gave him what background or conventional belief might have provided a more traditional-minded poet—a formal pattern and a method of restraint. Rationalism had deprived him of inherited values, and had left him a world in which experience could not be given order by relation to a received system. By seeing an event in terms of its opposite, Hardy gave it a significance independent of external reference; by setting two views of the event in juxtaposition he gave his poems form.

Irony also provided him with a defense against his greatest potential weakness—sentimentality. A sensitive man, aware of suffering and injustice in the world and lacking a traditional justification or explanation of them, is prone to an excessive reaction—the response to evil, when not balanced by a conviction of good, may be manifested in uncontrolled emotion. A purely literary tradition might have provided a classically trained poet with a sufficient restraint; but Hardy had not even that support. He had only the bare facts of his own observation, experience without referent. The antinomial pattern set a possible, if not always sufficient, curb to his compassion.

—Samuel Hynes. *The Pattern of Hardy's Poetry*. Chapel Hill, N.C.: The University of North Carolina Press (1961): 44–49.

WILLIAM H. PRITCHARD ON HARDY'S INVENTIVENESS

[William H. Pritchard is the author of *Playing it by Ear: Literary Essays and Reviews* (1994); *Randall Jarrell: A Literary Life* (1990); and *Frost: A Literary Life Reconsidered* (1993). In the following excerpt, Pritchard links Hardy's inventiveness in his treating of the Titanic disaster as both an "enlivened" discussion of human folly and a very personal commentary on his marriage to Emma Hardy.]

The domestic shadow which had passed over Hardy's head was the death of his wife in late November of 1912. During the next few months he wrote the remarkable "Poems of 1912–13," a group of eighteen lyrics (three more were added later) in response to that death. Although these are placed after the "Lyrics and Reveries" section of *Satires of Circumstances*, we can safely assume that he thought of them as prime examples of his "tenderest, least satirical verse," and that he worried about how his reputation as professional pessimist and "bitter" portrayer of life's little ironies might deform responses to what were very personal poems. Yet Macmillan's title was really the right one for the volume, and the 1912–13 lyrics are of great interest partly because they are not just tender, do not forego the strengths of his best satirical poetry.

But before taking up these poems and their biographical genesis, two of the most rightly anthologized of Hardy's works deserve attention as fine examples of the "public" poet's satiric strengths. "Channel Firing" and "The Convergence of the Twain" are the second and third poems in the "Lyrics and Reveries" section from *Satires of Circumstances*, but this heading fails to suggest the fabulous quality of each poem and the ambiguous way each reveals Hardy's presence. "Channel Firing" begins quietly and firmly with the voice of a dead man speaking from his coffin in rather four-square fashion:

That night your great guns, unawares,
Shook all our coffins as we lay,
And broke the chancel window-squares,
We thought it was the Judgment-day

And sat upright....

The man proceeds to relate how God had to reassure these dead
people that it was not in fact the Judgment-day but merely the
nations preparing for another war (Hardy dates the poem April,
1914), and that since the world was still mad they were not to get
their hopes up. At this news the dead subside, one of them,
Parson Thirdly, opining that instead of preaching he should have
"stuck to pipes and beer." So far it looks to be a satire of
circumstance in a familiar Hardyan vein, an exercise turned out
with perhaps too much facility. But the final stanza tolls its
message:

Again the guns disturbed the hour,
Roaring their readiness to avenge,
As far inland as Stourton Tower,
And Camelot, and starlit Stonehenge.

One of Hardy's very best critics, John Crowe Ransom, has nicely
pointed out how the meter makes us stress the "henge" in
Stonehenge. Ransom paraphrases the end of the poem this way:
"Our expectations have been defeated, but we still insist on our
moral universe; the roar of the guns prevails, but now it assaults
the shrines without effect"; and he concludes that "The thing
heard upon the air is evil, but the thing seen is the religious
monument hung and illuminated beneath the stars."

There is nothing in the poem that forbids this elegantly
humanistic way of understanding it; but suppose instead one
chose to emphasize, for the sake of discussion, how far the
roaring of the guns penetrated. As far as Camelot and
Stonehenge, a long way back in history and myth; thus one might
read the conclusion in a less affirmative way than Ransom does,
and might say instead "Look how far back war goes, learn how it
will ever be with us, realize how little there is you can do about

it." Different emphases are possible since all the poem's voice does is to declare, with rapt attentiveness and rhythmic power, what the guns are doing. But what everyone can agree about, I should think, is the sense of elevation—mainly through its use of romantic names, places and monuments—achieved by the final stanza, and perhaps felt by Hardy as he composed it. It may be that no statements about Man and War and History are as true as the juxtapositions and repetitions given expression here. Somehow the roaring of the guns ends up feeling dignified; and the reader may find himself entertaining some ennobling thoughts about war, rather than musing regretfully on the folly of mankind.

There is a similarly odd deflection from humanistic attitudes in his famous poem about the *Titanic* disaster. Much has been written in admiration of the marmoreal stanzas in which the great sunken ship is described:

> Over the mirrors meant
> To glass the opulent
> The sea-worm crawls—grotesque, slimed, dumb, indifferent

and through which Hardy, in explaining what happened, carefully prepares the coming together of the ship and its mate:

> And as the smart ship grew
> In stature, grace, and hue,
> In shadowy silent distance grew the Iceberg too.

The ending of the poem in which they meet, in which "consummation comes, and jars two hemispheres," is at the least a memorable one. But when we inquire about the reader's cumulative response, I think few would describe it as a sagely grave nodding at the ironical consequence of overwhelming pride and vanity. The "Convergence" is just too much fun to read for such responses seriously to exist; in fact it is but a slight overstatement to compare this poem with another utterance about the *Titanic* sinking, a song whose chorus ends with the ringing declaration "It was sad when that great ship went down" ("Husbands and wives / Little children lost their lives" etc.) to be boomed out with enthusiasm by communal singers who have drunk deep.

By designedly avoiding a personal, thoughtfully elaborated response to War or Disaster; by giving us instead such intricate constructions as "Channel Firing" or "Convergence of the Twain," Hardy appears as an ingenious, highly inventive entertainer, enlivened by the very examples of human folly which in life saddened or horrified him, as when he lost two acquaintances in the *Titanic* disaster. It comes as no surprise then to hear his second wife announce in a letter that her husband is upstairs, "writing an intensely dismal poem with great spirits." These facts may be born in mind when confronting the expressive sadness of "Poems of 1912–13."

—William H. Pritchard. "Hardy's Winter Words." *The Hudson Review*, vol. XXXII, no. 3 (Autumn 1979): 378–81.

PATRICIA CLEMENTS ON THE EXCLUSION OF CONSCIOUSNESS

[Patricia Clements is the author of *Baudelaire & the English Tradition* (1985) and an editor of *The Feminist Companion to Literature in English: Women Writers from the Middle Ages to the Present* (1990). In the following excerpt, Clements discusses the exclusion of consciousness in the "Convergence of the Twain."]

In 'A Commonplace Day' (78), 'The Contretemps' (539) and 'The Convergence of the Twain' (248), Hardy shows the order-hungry mind stylizing its experience. Each of these poems breaks into two, pivoting on a single word from a description in vivid particulars of an object or event to an abstract or figurative description of the same thing. The first half of 'A Commonplace Day', for instance, reports the end of a day which will 'join the anonymous host / Of those that throng oblivion'. Hardy presents the day's end in mere, brilliant particulars:

I part the fire-gnawed logs,
Rake forth the embers, spoil the busy flames, and lay the ends

Upon the shining dogs;
Further and further from the nooks the twilight's stride extends,
And beamless black impends.

The lines perfectly exemplify the point of the poem's first half: the day on which 'Nothing of tiniest worth' was achieved has only the value of its existence, now ending. But that thought awakens Hardy's 'regret', and on the repetition of that word he turns to consider what might have been the more than particular value of the day. His consideration transforms into metaphor the sensory particulars of the lines quoted above:

—Yet, maybe, in some soul,
In some spot undiscerned on sea or land, some impulse rose,
Or some intent upstole
Of that enkindling ardency from whose maturer glows
The world's amendment flows ....

'The Contretemps' (539), whose first five stanzas manage a plot of extreme, absurd complication, demonstrates a similar shift from particulars to pattern. It opens with an exquisite series of blunders: the speaker of the poem, rushing to an assignation, accidentally embraces a woman who, rushing to an assignation (but not with him) accidentally embraces him and so loses her husband and her lover, both of whom have observed the action and supposed themselves betrayed. The complications exemplify the chaos of an unplanned world, as is their purpose, and Hardy confirms his purpose in his imagery. The embrace itself is picked out of surrounding darkness by a 'lamp in the gloom'; and the vague air of a 'thawing brume' allows only the close-up details to be seen. The scene (one character is said to 'enter') is a 'lamplit, snowflaked, sloppiness'. The perspective is extremely narrow; the light prevents anything but the object from occupying the fovea.[18] In the sixth stanza, however, the poem draws back, unfolds an increasingly long view of the events it has presented. Its speaker becomes inward and accounts for his actions. His account transforms accident into romance, sloppiness into aesthetic shape:

So it began; and I was young,
    She pretty, by the lamp,
As flakes came waltzing down among
The waves of her clinging hair, that hung
Heavily on her temples, dark and damp.

As the 'twain hearts caught in one catastrophe' wonder what to do, Hardy slides them a step farther into fantasy, voicing their desire in the noise of the Jersey boat: '"One pairing is as good as another / Where all is venture! Take each other, / And scrap the oaths that you have aforetime made."' By the end of the poem, the incident of dramatic particulars has become illustrative, remote, an example of the general truth that 'Happiness comes in full to none'.

Like 'The Contretemps', 'The Convergence of the Twain' balances its two halves on the word, 'Well'. The word occurs in the sixth stanza:

Well: while was fashioning
This creature of cleaving wing,
The Immanent Will that stirs and urges everything

VII

Prepared a sinister mate
For her—so gaily great—
A Shape of Ice, for the time far and dissociate.

Unlike most of Hardy's poems, 'The Convergence of the Twain' is personless: the questing mind is explicitly excluded; the speaking voice is never personal. The shift in the middle of the poem, a brilliant chronological and stylistic leap, sets the elements of Hardy's central conflict into a kind of pure antithesis. On one side of his pivotal word, Hardy gives an account of the *Titanic* as object, remote from the 'Pride of Life that planned her', wrenched out of place in any design or pattern. Matter which had its sense in relation to mind is now mere matter, observed in its slow sea-changes by the 'sea-worm' and the 'Dim, moon-eyed fishes'. In the second half of the poem, Hardy submits that mere material to order. Reaching backwards in time, he finds the pattern of which the *Titanic*'s wreck is an item. She becomes now a part of the blind figure in the mind of the Immanent Will. Reporting pattern, Hardy shifts his style, transforms the direct, sensory language of the poem's first half into the figurative pattern of its second half. The sexual metaphor which is suggested in the sixth stanza is the poem's principle of organization by the seventh, racing to the end. After the pivotal 'Well' in this poem there is nothing *but* order.

'The Convergence of the Twain' perfects Hardy's irony. It sets mere object against mere pattern, dismantles the recurring conflict of his poems, and shows 'the sensuous mind' abused. In this poem, which is less about convergence than the division of matter from mind, Hardy excludes consciousness, blinds the mortal eye. Most of his poems make consciousness central: in them, the sensuous mind lives by preserving its conflicts, by repeatedly submitting its formalizations to correction in the fire of sensory apprehension.

NOTE

18. Cf. T.S. Eliot, 'Reflections on Contemporary Poetry', *The Egoist*, IV. 9 (Oct. 1917), p. 133.

> —Patricia Clements. *The Poetry of Thomas Hardy*, eds. Patricia Clements and Juliet Grindle. Totowa, N.J.: Barnes & Noble Books (1980): 151–54.

JOANNA CULLEN BROWN ON THE SENSUALITY OF "CONVERGENCE OF THE TWAIN"

[Joanna Cullen Brown is the editor of *Figures in a Wessex Landscape: Thomas Hardy's Picture of English Country Life* (1987) and *Let Me Enjoy the Earth: Thomas Hardy and Nature* (1990). In the following excerpt from her book, Brown discusses the sensuality of "Convergence of the Twain."]

Almost anyone else, called to write upon the *Titanic* disaster, would probably have evoked the suffering of the last scenes and the bereaved, perhaps the faults of the ship's design, possibly something about the massive forces of Nature ranged against human endeavour. Hardy's approach is uniquely his. From the first moment he sounds the note of human vanity, and by his quotation from the First Letter of John (Chapter 11, verse 16), sets an agenda which he proceeds to fill out imaginatively with a brilliant brush of sensuous imagery.

> For all that is in the world, the lust of the flesh, and the lust of the eyes, and the pride of life, is not of the Father, but is of the world.
> (1611 translation, "Authorised Version")

The eye travels slowly over the motionless wreck, as the ear catches the sea's gush and whine through the empty chambers, and one first senses the poles of cold and heat which vibrate throughout the poem. Here is the lust of the eyes unsatisfied— the seeing mirror slimed, the jewels blackened and dead, both recalling all those human expectations unfulfilled, blind and dumb and indifferent. The "moon-eyed fishes", suggests Jon Stallworthy, "in the necessary absence of the moon, embody the narrator's detached imagination, and into [their] mouths is put the question he must answer:

> 'What does this vaingloriousness down here?'"[24]

Well: almost exactly half-way through the poem, it turns (as often) on this one compendious word. The scene has been graphically set, in passive stillness disturbed only by the languid movements of sea-worm and fish, the ship "couched" in solitude as if awaiting her fate. Now, at the word "Well:" comes a sense of movement, of urgency, of purpose and fulfilment, which accelerates to the end of the poem. (I think of Donald Davie's description of Hardy as "the poet of technology, the laureate of engineering"—and this poem "like an engine, a sleek and powerful machine" whose rhymes "slide home like pistons in cylinders".)[25] But it is not just the rhymes that slide home. No longer described as a mere passive object, infiltrated by the sea, the ship is now seen as part of a purpose, "fashioned", in her feminine way, as the mate for that Shape of Ice which the urgent Immanent Will is preparing as her twin half ("a grim parody of the platonic symbol of perfection".)[26] The Shape is given "sinister" personality; the smart ship grows, like a woman, "in stature, grace and hue", and is a "creature of cleaving wing". The choice of "cleaving" was a late inspiration for Hardy, a flash of genius. Its overtones amplify the poem's meaning—overtones of "parting or dividing" (the water) and of "piercing or penetrating" as in the sexual metaphor and Biblical injunction to a man to "leave father and mother and ... cleave to his wife: and they twain shall be one flesh". It keeps too its simpler meaning of "to stick fast or adhere" which perfectly fits its relation to the iceberg.[27] The sexual metaphor implied from the beginning is continued in the word 'welding' as this wedding of Shape and gaily fashioned creature is prepared, a union of sinister Ice and created Fire in which it is the Ice which overcomes and turns her marriage into death. And as, below the surface, the iceberg penetrates the unconscious ship, the moment of consummation comes and meaning is made violently clear.

Hardy's change of tone and language in the second half—from passivity to urgency, from sensuous description to metaphorical and symbolic diction—is deliberately made to enhance the meaning. The first half conveys the picture of the aimless object on the seabed. The second half gathers up that object into the wider and deeper significance of the whole universe's pattern. Patricia Clements writes: "Reaching backwards in time, he finds the pattern of which the *Titanic's* wreck is an item. She becomes now a part of the blind figure in the mind of the Immanent Will."[28] Yet again Hardy is seeking to order the material of life to make meaning, to find reality.

But this poem is different in stance from his others in its total impersonality, its apparent negation of human consciousness and significance, so that the reader may feel excluded or uncomfortable. Stallworthy links its icy sterility with the "frigid circuit" of the moon poems. Patricia Clements calls it a poem "less about convergence than about the division of matter from mind." William Pritchard says that Hardy "spin[s] out an explanation that doesn't explain anything".[29] The poem is a living thing: like most of Hardy's poems, expressive of life's ambiguities, ironies, and inscrutabilities, and requiring an active and creative response from the reader, who must make of it what he or she will.

Notes

PTH   *The Poetry of Thomas Hardy*, ed Clements and Grindle (London 1980).
Agenda   Thomas Hardy Special Issue, Vol 10, Nos 2–3, 1972 ed Davie.

  24. *PTH*, 177.
  25. Donald Davie, *Thomas Hardy and British Poetry*, 17.
  26. Stallworthy, *PTH*, 177.
  27. Genesis II, 24; Matthew XIX, 5; Mark X, 7, etc. We must also note Jesus' emphasis on the word "twain" (A. V. translation). Definitions from the *OED*.
  28. *PTH*, 153.
  29. "Hardy's Anonymous Sincerity", *Agenda* 106.

     —Joanna Cullen Brown. *A Journey Into Thomas Hardy's Poetry*. London: W.H. Allen & Co Plc (1989): 295–7.

TIM ARMSTRONG ON FATE AND HUMAN ERROR

[Tim Armstrong is the author of *Modernism, Technology, and the Body: A Cultural Study* (1998) and editor of *Thomas Hardy: Selected Poems* (1993). In the following excerpt, Armstrong discusses Hardy's treatment of fate and human error in "Convergence of the Twain."]

In 'The Convergence of the Twain', Hardy describes the sinking of the *Titanic* as 'one august event'. Given the amount of literature surrounding the 'prediction' of the *Titanic* disaster, it is tempting to think that Hardy, one of the most etymologically informed of English poets, meant 'august' in its root sense of 'prepared by augury' and 'brought to fruition'. Indeed, as I will show, his poem seems to partake of the *Titanic* myth both in the popular sense in echoing a 'prediction' of the disaster, and in the more profound sense in suggesting that the potential for disaster was carried within the words that might be used to characterize such a ship, and within its particular impelling force or 'bent'. Hardy's poem, in part, questions the meaning of history and its apparent accidents.

After the sinking of the *Titanic*, the press was flooded with moralizing literature (Joseph Conrad, for example, wrote two pieces criticizing the 'monster ships' and the commercial values which produced them). Hardy's poem, first published as a part of the souvenir programme for a charity event in aid of a disaster fund, was part of that literature. But it was not without its own antecedents, perhaps even a model.[8] In the issue for the week ending 20 April 1912, the *Spectator* published a letter by B. Paul Newman containing a poem called 'A Tryst', which described a ship and an iceberg with a 'dread appointment':

> Sir,—I do not know whether you care to print the enclosed poem by Celia Thaxter, an American poetess, who is, I am afraid, little known on this side of the Atlantic. It was published more than thirty years ago in the *Atlantic Monthly*.... It tells of a disaster less terrible, though more complete; than that which has befallen the 'Titanic'.[9]

Indeed this poem by a New England maritime poet, the daughter of a lighthouse keeper, did seem oddly prophetic, and it sparked off what threatened to turn into a literary competition in the *Spectator* as rival anticipations of the wreck were found in De Quincey, Kipling, and elsewhere.

Hardy's poem could almost be another contribution to the *Spectator* (in which he published poems in the 1910s). The timing is tight: there would have been a little over a week between the *Spectator*'s coming out and Hardy's date of composition, 24 April, but it is entirely likely that the weeklies were read avidly in the weeks following the disaster. The similarity of the scheme of his poem to Thaxter's is striking. Both posit the ship and iceberg as thesis and antithesis and alternate descriptions of them; both picture a version of Fate watching the scene. (...)

Hardy's answer to the question of what 'caused' the disaster that is the occasion of the poem at first seems implicitly 'Theistic', linked to the Immanent Will which watches and 'prepares' events. There is a hint of the moralizing typical of *Titanic* literature in his references to 'human vanity' and 'Pride of Life', derived from Ecclesiastes and 1 John 2:16, and the latter allusion suggests that what the Apostle calls the 'lust of the eyes' and the excessively worldly extravagance of the ship produce a chastisement, a moral lesson imposed from without. The ironic rhymes reinforce this bitter conclusion about the fate of a latter-day Ship of Fools: opulent/indifferent; mind/blind. That the *Titanic* was a piece of Vanity was a lesson universally drawn, by a range of public opinion from the Bishops to Conrad and the popular press. Moreover, as Jeremy Hawthorn points out, Hardy distances himself from more material explanations of the disaster, abstracting it away from the issues of speed, signalling, lifeboat provision which were to occupy the official inquiries, and offering what seems a meditation on 'timeless' absolutes.[15]

But Hardy is also interested in investigating more deeply, in looking at the process through which such a moral lesson might be suggested: the simple contrast between sunken opulence and a 'creature of cleaving wing' is not sufficient. The second half of the poem, couched as it is in ambiguous terms which might be seen to both offer and withdraw a sense of active forces at work, raises more interesting questions about where responsibility is to be placed:

> Well: while was fashioning
> This creature of cleaving wing,
> The Immanent Will that stirs and urges everything
>
> Prepared a sinister mate
> For her—so gaily great—
> A Shape of Ice, for the time far and dissociate.

The unusual participle suggests that what happens merely happens: 'was fashioning' implies an absent subject ('[the Immanent Will] was fashioning'), but then withdraws it; it is not the Immanent Will that fashions the ship, not even mankind or the White Star Line seemingly, but just a process of 'being fashioned'. Nevertheless, the use of the Immanent Will does suggest a force behind history, and the allusions to angel and archangel, type and anti-type, sexual fusion and Platonic halves, place the event within a discernible pattern—even though at this point 'No mortal eye could see', as he puts it, 'the intimate welding of their later history.' 'Welding' is one of Hardy's jokes, referring to the construction of ships, but it also raises the question of whether the ship's fate is welded into it by its makers, or whether the welding is imposed from without by the Immanent Will. The stanza which follows is equally ambiguous with respect to agency. Hardy first wrote:

> And so coincident
> In course as to be meant
> To form anon twin halves of one august event,

where 'meant' seems to be the imposition of Fate. But the poem as revised for the *Fortnightly Review* and in its final version was more ambiguous, saying 'Or sign that they were bent / By paths coincident / On being anon'. 'Bent' can be either active or passive here: it seems at first to suggest an outside force that they were 'bent / By'. But then, in the third line of the stanza, the arrival of the adverbial preposition 'on' seems to alter that, indicating that the ships themselves have an embodied will, being 'bent on' collision—an interpretation which suggests Comte's 'Fetishistic' universe of self-motivated objects. Was the collision willed by or somehow built into the *Titanic* itself? Or was it simply Fate? There is a systematic uncertainty at work within these lines, what we could call a 'bent by / bent on' principle which permeates them. The words used to describe the ship also carry a number of ambiguities. The ship is described as 'smart', that is elegant, neat, and perhaps also brisk, alert. David Perkins suggests that 'smart' here 'may be pejorative', and indeed it is: the word has associations of hurt, and even, as the *Oxford English Dictionary* puts it, of 'suffering of the nature of punishment or retribution' ('smart-money' is the money paid to widows of seamen).[16] The adjective thus carries a hint of the ship's destiny. 'August' in the phrase 'august event' can mean, as I have said, either grand or predicted and ripened, as if one should have known what was going to happen. We might even see a quibble on 'anon': was it, or was it not, an anonymous deed? Once again, are disasters caused or accidental? 'Anon' is curious: it means 'soon' of course, but that would be redundant in this context, except for filling out the metre. Perhaps Hardy is also thinking of the older meaning suggested by the Old English roots *on an* and *on ane*, a unity 'in one body, mind, state, act, way, course, motion, movement, moment', as the *Oxford English Dictionary* climactically phrases it. In that case, the word itself recapitulates the argument: their being 'anon twin halves' means that they are fated to be coincident. The only question, as in all discussions of fate, is that of the 'moment'; it is a matter of waiting,

> Till the Spinner of the Years
> Said 'Now!' And each one hears,
> And consummation comes, and jars two hemispheres.

The ambiguity about agency is retained by this Pataphysical 'explanation' (an example of Alfred Jarry's 'science of imaginary solutions'). The string of three 'ands' seems more like a Humean constant conjunction than the actions suggested by the verb of command ('then' would imply a different effect). The word 'consummation', with its biblical overtones, again suggests typological thinking, but once more the indirect construction weakens the sense of agency: not 'it is consummated' but 'consummation comes', through the back door as it were. At this point, the perspective of Hardy (and the reader) is curiously like that of the Immanent Will, merely watching what has been set in motion. Agency seems to have been offered, only to be removed, or rather be made an effect of the text, something hidden in the words of the poem rather than embodied in its personified first cause. Even Hardy's revision of the name of that entity suggests a qualification: the term he first wrote, 'Mover', implies implosion, while 'Spinner', while it fits in with a pattern of Shelleyan imagery which permeates Hardy's poetry, also suggests an aesthetic effect more like the work of the writer than that of a 'Mover', an effect only perceptible once the pattern is finished. As language is 'animated' (to borrow Comte's phrase), History becomes art. (…)

'The Convergence of the Twain' has two entities usually regarded as being effectively the same: the 'Immanent Will' and the 'Spinner of the Years'. But in one crucial respect they are different. The Immanent Will acts, but like its counterpart in *The Dynasts* it is silent. The 'Spinner of the Years' seems to me to be closer to the Spirit of the Pities (and to Hardy himself) through having a voice which marks, rather than simply impelling, the consummation which 'comes'. Hardy's view of history is similarly divided between the desire for an agent within history, and a recognition of the fact that the idea of agency as an imposed direction (a 'curve' or 'run') is bound up with human hopes, expectations, and recognitions, always belated and subject to accident. His poem suggests that there are two ways of looking at what happened to the *Titanic*. In one, its sinking was a chastisement of mankind prepared by the Immanent Will and inflicted on the ship. In this view of things, which, as we saw, the poem initially seems to support (and moralize), 'history' is an abstract entity like that which the Idealist tradition postulates, 'bending' human fate. In the other way of looking at things, however, the sinking of the *Titanic* was not the action of a Will, but rather was built into it, not so much by the builders, who are unconscious of what they do, but by Hardy himself, in the words which describe it in his own poem and trace its career as he watches and marks like the 'Spinner of the Years'. In this view, history is always the product of the interaction of human efforts and designs, and ultimately of the act of interpretation itself and the tropes used to describe it (a trope being itself a kind of 'bending' or 'welding' of words).

NOTES

8. I am, here, setting aside other possible influences on Hardy's poem, such as R. S. Hawker's 'The Fatal Ship'.

9. *Spectator*, 20 April 1912, p. 620. Thaxter wrote extensively on marine subjects; she ran a hotel on Appledore Island, New Hampshire, frequented by the Transcendentalists.

15. Jeremy Hawthorn, *Cunning Passages: New Historicism, Cultural Materialism and Marxism in the Contemporary Literary Debate* (London: Arnold, 1996), pp. 109–24.

16. David Perkins, *A History of Modern Poetry: From the 1890s to the High Modernist Mode* (Cambridge, MA: Belknap Press, 1976), p. 151. While Perkins writes that 'nothing follows from the sinking of the *Titanic*; no moral is drawn', it seems to me that the conventional moral is clearly drawn in the opening section.

—Tim Armstrong. *Haunted Hardy: Poetry, History, Memory*. Houndmills, Basingstoke, Hampshire and New York: Palgrave (2000): 113–14; 119–21 and 124–5.

"The Darkling Thrush"

"The Darkling Thrush" was first published in the *Graphic* on December 29, 1900, entitled "By Century's Deathbed." With the "Century's corpse outleant," it announced on the central themes of this poem, a commentary upon the dying century, to be read as if written as darkness fell on the last day of 1899. However, as Hardy's original manuscript indicates that its present title "The Darkling Thrush" had always been his intention and, indeed, many connotations adhere as a result. Though at first it appears that the poet is inviting the reader to join him in his contemplation of the countryside on the last day of the century as he listens to the thrush's "full-hearted evensong," the title of the poem undermines its rustic simplicity by suggesting that it be read in the context of literary tradition. The word "darkling" is a poetic word with the general meaning of "shrouded in darkness" and has an impressive literary inheritance. In *Paradise Lost*, the blind poet, compares inspiration to a "wakeful Bird / [that] Sings darkling, and in shadiest Covert hid," suggesting the flow of music more from feeling. Keats also associates poetic inspiration with the nightingale as he listens "darkling" to its intoxicating song ("Ode to a Nightingale"). Finally, Shelley's influence on "The Darkling Thrush" has received a good deal of critical attention. In "Ode to the West Wind" (1819), in which the poet prays to the West Wind, wishing to partake of its poetic powers, he likewise depicts the "pestilent-stricken" landscape of "the dying year." Most especially, with respect to Keats and Shelley, a crisis of imagination is expressed in which the inspirational powers of Nature are invoked as the means of transcending the feeling of belatedness and inferiority. "The Darkling Thrush" participates in that poetic tradition as both the reworking of the conventional elegy for purposes of meditating on literary matters at the dawn of the twentieth century and as a wish for his own poetic regeneration.

The first stanza posits a bleak and depressing landscape as the speaker leans on the "coppice gate" and surveys the dismal scene.

Indeed, the scene is devoid of all forms of life, both natural and human. All that remains is a cold and colorless world, "spectre-gray," rendered nondescript and featureless by "the weakening eye of day." Even worse, the very memory of its former inhabitants has now been obliterated. "And all mankind that haunted nigh / Had sought their household fires." But, most importantly, the joy and harmony of Nature have also departed, where only "tangled bine-stems" of a previously vibrant plant remain, "like strings of broken lyres," mute symbols of a time as far back as the ancient world when poetry and music were one, now become feeble reminders of their former exalted status.

> "It is not surprising that poets should wish to keep hold of an association with song which goes back to the very origins of their art, and which carries with it such powerful connotations of divine authority, potency, and vision. My argument is that the wish became an anxiety during a period which begins, very roughly, with Milton, and ends with a group of poets who straddle the end of the nineteenth century and the beginning of the twentieth.... Why this loss of empire happened is a fascinating and complex story, far to complex to analyze here ... Nevertheless, I think it is no coincidence that poets insisted on identifying themselves—self-consciously, rhetorically—as *singers* at a historical moment of divergence between poetry and song....
>
> (Danny Karlin,
> "The Figure of the Singer in the Poetry of Thomas Hardy")

Amidst this barren background, in the second stanza the poet laments the death of the nineteenth century by endowing it with human attributes, "the Century's corpse outleant," and conceiving a funeral service attended only by the all but defunct forces of nature. Here, the wind no longer produces the sweet music of the lyre but, rather, provides the funeral dirge. "His crypt the cloudy canopy, / The wind his death-lament." Instead, the promise of renewed inspiration, "the ancient pulse if germ and birth," is buried in a wasteland that reflects the poet's dejected state of mind. "And every spirit upon earth / Seemed fervourless as I." It is important to note that the last two lines of this stanza indicate an important reversal in terms of cause and effect with respect to nature and the poet's state of mind. Up to this point, the poet has presented himself as depressed by his surroundings, whereas now he suggests that the landscape is a mirror for his feelings, merely reflecting back to him his own sense of lost creativity. Thus, a poem which at first appears to describe a rustic (NW) landscape is transformed into one that uses the guise of Nature to express the poet's emotional struggle.

Having buried the past century and his poetic precursors, the third stanza suggests that there is yet some hope that the poet may find a way out of his dilemma when he overhears the song of "an aged thrush." It appears at first that there is indeed a way of resolving his crisis as he listens to its "full-hearted evensong / Of joy illimited," where happiness without boundaries signals the successful transcendence of his previous fears and anxiety. The poet imagines the thrush coming to his rescue, having "chosen to fling his soul / Upon the growing gloom." But for all this, the poet's desire for a renewed sense of well-being is not assured for he is imagining an aged bird with "blast-beruffled plume."

More importantly, the poet cannot participate in the thrush's celebratory mood for he cannot imagine any reason for its happiness. This is the theme of the fourth and final stanza. Here, the poet simply cannot find any reason for hope or any way out of his crisis. When he states that he cannot imagine any "cause for carolings / Of such ecstatic sound," we are made to understand that he can no longer be inspired by the sound of the thrush's singing, unable to identify with or be transported by its music. His imaginative efforts to the contrary, the poet simply cannot find a way out of his feelings of futility and hopelessness. "Some blessed Hope, whereof he knew / And I was unaware."

"The Darkling Thrush"

MERRYN WILLIAMS ON THE INFLUENCE OF KEATS AND SHELLEY

[Merryn Williams is the author of *Thomas Hardy and Rural England* (1972); *Women in the English Novel, 1800-1900* (1984); and *Margaret Oliphant: A Critical Biography* (1986). In the following excerpt, Williams discusses the influence of Keats and Shelley on "The Darkling Thrush."]

In between these two poems, Hardy wrote one that is entirely different:

The Darkling Thrush

I leant upon a coppice gate
  When Frost was spectre-gray,
And Winter's dregs made desolate
  The weakening eye of day.
The tangled bine-stems scored the sky
  Like strings of broken lyres,
And all mankind that haunted nigh
  Had sought their household fires.

The land's sharp features seemed to be
  The Century's corpse outleant,
His crypt the cloudy canopy,
  The wind his death-lament.
The ancient pulse of germ and birth
  Was shrunken hard and dry,
And every spirit upon earth
  Seemed fervourless as I.

At once a voice arose among
  The bleak twigs overhead
In a full-hearted evensong
  Of joy unlimited;

An aged thrush, frail, gaunt, and small
  In blast-beruffled plume,
Had chosen thus to fling his soul
  Upon the growing gloom.

So little cause for carolings
  Of such ecstatic sound
Was written on terrestrial things,
  Afar or nigh around,
That I could think there trembled through
  His happy good-night air
Some blessed Hope, whereof he knew
  And I was unaware.

DATE This poem was first published in the last days of 1900, under the title 'By the Century's Deathbed'.

STYLE AND LITERARY BACKGROUND Nobody else could conceivably have written this poem, yet it owes a good deal to two masterpieces by the younger Romantics, Keats's 'Ode to a Nightingale' and Shelley's 'To a Skylark'. Hardy knew both these poems well, and 'The Darkling Thrush' is written from the same point of view. In all three poems, the bird's song reveals a new, mysterious and joyful world to the poet, who is deeply unhappy and dissatisfied with the world as it is. Keats, listening to the nightingale, wishes to 'leave the world unseen / And with thee fade away into the forest dim',

Fade far away, dissolve, and quite forget
  What thou among the leaves has never known,
The weariness, the fever, and the fret,
  Here, where men sit and hear each other groan;
Where palsy shakes a few, sad, last gray hairs,
  Where youth grows pale, and spectre-thin, and dies;
    Where but to think is to be full of sorrow
      And leaden-eyed despairs;
Where Beauty cannot keep her lustrous eyes,
  Or new Love pine at them beyond tomorrow.

Shelley also feels that the skylark is living in a much happier state than human beings can ever reach:

Yet if we could scorn
Hate, and pride, and fear;
If we were things born
Not to shed a tear,
I know not how thy joy we ever should come near.

Unhappiness, a feeling of deadness and desolation, is the point from which Hardy begins 'The Darkling Thrush'. The first two verses show a landscape on a winter evening, which mirrors the 'fervourless' state of the poet's mind. In the third verse, and quite unexpectedly, he suddenly hears the thrush 'fling his soul / Upon the growing gloom'. The language is similar to that of Keats, who imagines the nightingale 'pouring forth thy soul abroad / In such an ecstasy' (the thrush is 'ecstatic' too). Yet the overall impression of this poem is quite different from that of Keats's, or Shelley's. Shelley imagines the singing bird as a 'blithe spirit', 'an unbodied joy', or 'a star of heaven in the broad daylight' (it is significant that he cannot actually see it). The nightingale in the Keats ode is also invisible, an ethereal being which was 'not born for death'. Both of them seem unaware that this arvelous music actually comes from a little, ordinary bird. Hardy, on the other hand, can see the bird clearly:

An aged thrush, frail, gaunt, and small,
In blast-beruffled plume.

This bird obviously is born for death. It is old, frail, and knocked about by the winter winds, yet this does not destroy the core of happiness which makes it sing.

Although, as we noted, some expressions in this poem (including the word 'darkling') were suggested by the Keats ode, this is a deliberately plain and simple piece of work which keeps well clear of the 'poetic' imagery used by the two earlier writers. 'I leant upon a coppice-gate' is very different, as an opening line, from 'Hail to thee, blithe spirit!', and this is characteristic of Hardy's writing.

SUBJECT   We know that the 1890s were a bad time for Hardy, with the attacks on his last two novels and troubled marriage (and if we didn't know, we could guess it from 'In Tenebris' and 'Wessex Heights'). He must also have felt that the nineteenth century had been a time of terrible human suffering, bearing in mind that the South African war was being fought as he wrote. This tended to make him feel that the only way to live without being hurt was in a state of 'unhope'. In this frame of mind he becomes aware of the thrush, which is singing joyfully as the landscape grows darker, although for no apparent reason:

> So little cause for carolings
>   Of such ecstatic sound
> Was written on terrestrial things
>   Afar or nigh around.

The thrush, then, seems to know about 'some blessed Hope' of which the poet is 'unaware'. Some critics have thought that this 'blessed Hope' must be God. Perhaps, but then Hardy had always believed that human life contained hopeful elements (this poem is never cited by those who call him a pessimist). He had shown how the same thing happened to Tess Durbeyfield, after her 'fall': 'Some spirit within her rose automatically as the sap in the twigs. It was unexpended youth, surging up anew after its temporary check, and bringing with it hope, and the invincible instinct towards self-delight'. It is this 'invincible instinct towards self-delight' which makes the thrush sing, just as it makes the sap rise (Hardy describes how 'the ancient pulse of germ and birth / Was shrunken hard and dry', but we can scarcely doubt that, in spring, it will begin all over again). Hardy's point seems to be that the bleakest of lives can still offer sources of happiness, even if this is only the song of an elderly thrush.

> —Merryn Williams. *A Preface to Hardy*. Essex, UK: Pearson Education Limited (1993): 150–53.

JOHN BAYLEY ON HARDY'S TREATMENT OF BIRDS

[John Bayley is the author of *The Short Story: Henry James to Elizabeth Bowen* (1988); *Elegy for Iris* (1999) and *Iris and* her *Friends: A Memoir of Memory and Desire* (2000). In the following excerpt from his essay, Bayley discusses Hardy's treatment of birds.]

The Darkling Thrush was no doubt a relief to them all (as Hardy records) but it is actually the same kind of poem. Despite Hardy's extreme interest in ideas and new theories, the objects of his imagination remained obstinately unaware of public opinion and the climate of change. How much so can be shown by another reference to *Church Going*, and its concluding lines. 'A serious house on serious earth it is', because human needs are realizeed there and cannot grow obsolete:

> Since someone will forever be surprising
> A hunger in himself to be more serious,
> And gravitating with it to this ground,
> Which, he once heard, was proper to grow wise in,
> If only that so many dead lie round.

Like many of Larkin's it seems a poem very much akin to Hardy, but its success in fact depends on a totally different tone. This is concentrated in the word 'serious', used of an instinct which still attracts people towards a church, which has nothing to do with belief, indeed is 'what remains when disbelief has gone'. The poem is faintly ironic about this reaction and yet wholly sympathetic to it, a combination in its quiet way highly collusive with the reader and rather flattering to him. We are dispossessed but sensitive people, humorous about our losses and our persisting nostalgias. In the metre and cadence there is an echo of *The Scholar Gipsy*, also a collusive poem with a wryly humorous note behind it, not so much in its tone as in the way it draws us into the higher intimacy with Matthew Arnold, as kindred souls who know and perceive as he does.

No wonder Hardy was not able to persuade readers into this kind of intimacy, and make them smile regretfully with him. Larkin's humour, and perhaps Arnold's too, is subtly successful in committing the reader to it before disclosing itself. It makes us realize how intimate is the kind of poetry with which Hardy seems to have most in common—going back to Wordsworth and

Cowper; and how careful to keep its tone, especially its humorous tone, such poetry usually is, even to the point of gratifying, as Larkin's does, 'known habits of association'. For better or worse, Hardy is always independent of such intimacy. His verbal peculiarities are of course predictable—Max Beerbohm did an excellent verse parody—but his tone never quite is.

The thrush, for instance, crops up again in a comic poem about one who has been caught by men, and hopes to learn from them—'How happy days are made to be'. But, escaped back to the other birds, he has to report that this secret:

> Eludes great Man's sagacity
> No less than ours, O tribes in treen!
> Men know but little more than we
> How happy days are made to be.

As the portable ambiguity (made by whom?) suggests in the refrain, Hardy enjoyed the 'scrabble' possibilities of the repetitions in these verse forms. In another, the villanelle becomes an exceedingly ingenious triolet—

> Around the house the flakes fly faster
> And all the berries now are gone
> From holly and cotone-aster
> Around the house. The flakes fly—faster
> Shutting indoors that crumb-outcaster
> We used to see upon the lawn
> Around the house. The flakes fly faster,
> And all the berries now are gone.

Larkin follows Hardy in having joke poems among the serious ones, but Hardy uses just the same sort of anthropomorphism in poems of all kinds, thus further confounding and cutting off the reader's expectations. The birds are treated as 'unseriously' as religion, a fact all the more evident if we recall a famous poem of Sassoon, another of Hardy's admirers—'Everyone suddenly burst out singing'. It is an emotional poem, the reader's emotion readily following the poet's into the region where

My heart was shaken with tears, and horror
Drifted away

and where inarticulate beauty and a benighted world are all of a
piece. The poem movingly succeeds, but in its atmosphere of
wistfulness and elevation Hardy's ingenuities about feeding birds
or talking birds would be quite out of the question.

The point seems to be that nothing is expected by Hardy of
his animistic fancies: sometimes he attaches weight to them and
sometimes they act as a playful statement. He and the poem are
happy either way.

—John Bayley. *An Essay on Hardy*. London and New: Cambridge
University Press (1978): 51–54.

Geoffrey Harvey on "The Darkling Thrush" as a Modern Lament

[Geoffrey Harvey is the author of *The Complete Critical
Guide to Thomas Hardy* (2003) and "Thomas Hardy's Poetry
of Transcendence" (1978). In the following excerpt, Harvey
discusses "The Darkling Thrush" as a "modern lament for
the death of God and of nature."]

As Donald Davie has pointed out, there is no clear line of
development in Hardy's verse.[15] His major visionary poems
occur sporadically throughout his career because the unfettered
operation of his poetic will was a rare accident, dependent on his
sense of equilibrium in the universe. This feeling permeates 'The
Darkling Thrush', for instance, a poem of the highest
imaginative order. Apparently a modern lament for the death of
God and of nature, the poem employs a niversalized and
visionary landscape to record the end of place and time:

I leant upon a coppice gate
    When Frost was spectre-gray,
And Winter's dregs made desolate
    The weakening eye of day.

The tangled bine-stems scored the sky
　　Like strings of broken lyres,
And all mankind that haunted nigh
　　Had sought their household fires.

The land's sharp features seemed to be
　　The Century's corpse outleant,
His crypt the cloudy canopy,
　　The wind his death-lament.
The ancient pulse of germ and birth
　　Was shrunken hard and dry,
And every spirit upon earth
　　Seemed fervourless as I.

This awful nullity, which is developed in the image patterns of
the first two stanzas, is mirrored in the consciousness of the poet
himself. The century's outleant corpse makes a parallel with the
poet who 'leant upon a coppice gate', the 'weakening eye of day'
creates a metaphor for the darkened vision of the poet, while the
tangled bine-stems scoring the sky 'Like strings of broken lyres'
is a further image of poetic sterility. The poet stands in mute
contrast to the joyous thrush, the only other inhabitant of this
ghastly landscape, and to the creative impulse of the bird's 'full-
hearted' song:

At once a voice arose among
　　The bleak twigs overhead
In a full-hearted evensong
　　Of joy illimited;
An aged thrush, frail, gaunt, and small,
　　In blast-beruffled plume,
Had chosen thus to fling his soul
　　Upon the growing gloom.

So little cause for carolings
　　Of such ecstatic sound
Was written on terrestrial things
　　Afar or nigh around,
That I could think there trembled through
　　His happy good-night air

Some blessed Hope, whereof he knew
	And I was unaware.

Hardy's central distinction, between the poetic sterility of the man, for whom the universe is dead, and the thrush which experiences hope and joy, appears to justify Hillis Miller's criticism of Hardy as a detached and passive observer whose poetry displays a fundamental withdrawal from life. But this view does not do justice to the complexity of the poem. Here, as in several of his visionary poems, Hardy inhabits the world of the poem not only as a neutral spectator, but also as an active participant. This duality of experience is embodied in the structure of the poem, which creates a profound connection between the two inhabitants of its desolate world, the nihilistic poet and the optimistic thrush. Of course the thrush has a richly symbolic function. On one level its instinctive song represents the natural world's anticipation of spring and regeneration. It is also a niversalized symbol of humanity. But fundamentally, 'aged', 'frail, gaunt, and small', like the poet himself, the thrush functions in the poem as its governing symbol for the continued creative activity of the poetic will, which is still at work below the level of conscious thought, and which is free to operate because the temporal frame of the poem crystalises a moment of poise in the universe. Like the poet, who is both observer and agent, the thrush creates his essential self by means of an act of will; he has '*chosen* thus to fling his soul / Upon the growing gloom' (emphasis added)—a defiant action, which images his attempt to transcend the way he has been 'thrown' into the world in an existential sense. The thrush's affirmation of the sheer joy of being in the present moment, and the accompanying sense of significance, are given peculiar force by the poem's terrible context of non-being, and by the awful irony of the poetic *persona*'s inability to grasp the meaning offered. Nevertheless, its song of ecstatic optimism, an unwitting act of loving-kindness, forges a contact between itself and the poet, creating a sense of his solidarity with all living things; and, because the thrush also represents the enduring connection between the poet and his creative imagination, the poem is allowed to stand as a courageous celebration of the poetic will, and of the possibility for the survival of undeceived joy in a world of dissolution.

NOTE

15. Davie, *Thomas Hardy and British Poetry*, p. 28.

—Geoffrey Harvey. *The Romantic Tradition in Modern English Poetry: Rhetoric and Experience*. New York: St. Martin's Press (1986): 53–55.

ROBERT LANGBAUM ON HARDY'S RESPONSE TO KEATS AND SHELLEY

[Robert Langbaum is the author of *The Word from Below: Essays on Modern Literature and Culture* (1987) and *The Poetry of Experience: The Dramatic Monologue in Modern Literary Tradition* (1985). In the following excerpt, Langbaum discusses "The Darkling Thrush" as Hardy's response to Keats and Shelley.]

Instead of romantic projection, Hardy often uses the traditional devices of allegory and personification to make nature yield meaning. In 'The Darkling Thrush', the landscape becomes 'The [Nineteenth] Century's corpse outleant' (I: 187). In 'Hap' (1866), Hardy realises that 'Crass Casualty' would strew 'blisses' in my path as readily as the 'pain' I encounter (I: 10) so that design of any kind, even malevolent design, would be a consolation. Although a later poem 'The Subalterns' (1901) makes the opposite point—that life seems less grim when the speaker realises that Cold, Sickness and Death are like himself helpless agents of natural laws (I: 155)—both poems insist on nature's indifference. Here and elsewhere Hardy's blatant anthropomorphism, as compared to Wordsworth's gentle animation of nature, indicates how utterly *non*-anthropomorphic nature really is. Only the self-referentiality of Hardy's artificial rhetoric can convey the meaning of meaninglessness. (...)

I have already shown how Hardy sums up and writes finis to the Victorian period in 'An Ancient to Ancients'. He does an equally powerful summing up of romanticism in his most capitalized poem 'The Darkling Thrush', dated 31 December 1900. The title recalls Keats's 'Ode to a Nightingale', in which the poet listens 'darkling' to the bird singing in the dark wood. 'When Frost was spectre-gray' recalls Keats's 'spectre-thin' youth, and the thrush who has chosen 'to fling his soul' forth 'In a full-hearted evensong / Of joy illimited' recalls both Keats's nightingale 'pouring forth thy soul abroad / In such an ecstasy!' and Shelley's skylark who 'Pourest thy full heart / ... Like an unbodied joy'. The earlier birds, however, did not like Hardy's fling their songs upon a *resistant* 'growing gloom' (Keats's dark wood is penetrable, it intensifies the sensuous imagination). The most poignant contrast is in Hardy's lines, 'The tangled bine-stems scored the sky / Like strings of broken lyres' (I: 187–8) which, as John Bayley points out, recall Shelley's 'Ode to the West Wind': 'Make me thy lyre, even as the forest is' (*Essay on Hardy*, 37). By 1900 the sky shows through the tangled bine-stems and the poet's lyre is broken. The climactic irony occurs in the third stanza where we learn to our surprise that the song comes from 'An aged thrush, frail, gaunt, and small', who is unbodied, not because like Shelley's skylark and Keats's nightingale it is too ethereal or poetic to be visible, but because its body has been wasted by age and struggle against a hostile environment. Here is Hardy's realistic comment on romantic poetry.

Behind the whole poem stands Wordsworth, who is recalled by the Lucy poems' quatrains and by a waste land imagery—'The ancient pulse of germ and birth / Was shrunken hard and dry'— that reverses the vitality of Wordsworth's landscapes. Wordsworth's poetic method is reversed by the split between the description of the landscape and the meaning imposed upon it through allegory not projection. The lines, 'The land's sharp features seemed to be / The Century's corpse outleant', recall the original allegorical title, 'By the Century's Deathbed', when the poem first appeared in the *Graphic* on December 29. It is a sign of the poet's non-projectiveness that the thrush's joyful song makes no headway against 'the growing gloom', or as Bayley says, 'It is because the pathetic fallacy is so absolute that the thrush and his song remain wholly outside it' (39).

The first three stanzas move like major poetry through a steady intensification of the imagery and irony. But in the fourth and last stanza Hardy retreats to minor poetry by shrugging off the impasse he posed, with in the last two lines a pat remark the very rhythm of which is trivial as compared to the rhythm of the previous stanzas' concluding lines. 'So little cause for carolings', he reflects,

> That I could think there trembled through
>   His happy good-night air
> Some blessed Hope, whereof he knew
>   And I was unaware.
>
> (I: 188)

The thrush's song is so distinctly unrelated to the landscape and the poet's feelings that the capitalized Hope emerges as the poet's wishful fancy, a sentimentally optimistic interpretation incongruent with the preceding ideas but which probably accounts for the poem's popularity.

We find another realistic comment on romanticism in 'Shelley's Skylark' which reminds us that the bird Shelley hails as 'blithe Spirit! / Bird thou never wert' was now 'A pinch of unseen, unguarded dust' that 'only lived like another bird, / And knew not its immortality'. He thinks of the bird's death, when it fell one day, 'A little ball of feather and bone' and of its biological continuance through the food chain. Only faeries, he concludes—changing direction by praising Shelley's transforming imagination—could find 'That tiny pinch of priceless dust' and lay it in 'a casket silver-lined'; for the poem not the bird is immortal (I: 133). Given his uncomfortable unawareness of the disjunction between the real bird and what Shelley made of it, Hardy would not and could not write such an immortal poem, but this inability, we are to understand, is a disadvantage. It's just that Hardy as poet must take into account commonplace facts. 'The point is (in imaginative literature)', Hardy wrote in his notebook, 'to adopt that form of romanticism which is the mood of the age' (*Life*, 147).

—Robert Langbaum. *Thomas Hardy in Our Time*. New York: St. Martin's Press, Inc. (1995): 45 and 51–3.

BRIAN GREEN ON THE SPEAKER'S EMOTIONAL STATE

[Brian Green is the author of "Darkness Visible: Defiance, Derision and Despair in Hardy's 'In Tenebris' Poems" (1990) and "A Sun for His Soul: Worth, Wonder, and Warmth in Hardy's Lyrics" (1994). In the following excerpt, Green discusses the relationship of imagery in "The Darkling Thrush" to the speaker's mental and emotional state in the final stanza.]

Far subtler in its affirmation of the instincts for human dignity,; wonder and warmth is the ostensibly occasional poem 'The Darkling Thrush'. First, 'Darkling' means not simply 'in the dark' or 'obscure', but the emotional experience of that dark. The word has connotations, if not specifically of 'despair and the burden of the past'[9], then more generally of the stealing in of a mournful heavy-heartedness. Then, the artificed title encapsulates the overall structure and mood of the poem. The title dynamically counterpoints the speaker's observation of the spritely bird reduced to frailty by seasonal vicissitude with the same speaker's assertive interpretation of the bird's song as joyful. This oxymoronic effect of the title, suggestive of the diminution of the zest and potential for growth, is enforced by the allusiveness of the literary epithet. Yet, while 'darkling' may well recall and rely on the rich experience of English culture embodied in great works of poetry, the intertextual resonance also registers the ironical waning of the significance of all that accumulated experience, the recent demise of an entire era of human achievement and failure, since Hardy first entitled the poem 'By the Century's Deathbed'. For the central tension Hardy ecognize in the poem is that between traditional and individual quests for significance. Everything is seen through the eyes of the speaker; and it is he alone who interprets as an expression of joy the sound the bird makes. Hardy uses the literary allusion to suggest an ultimate bleakness and meaninglessness that is the precise objective context in which the humanist speaker creates significance out of his own humanity.[10]

After taking 'a full look at the Worst', at the scenic desolation and cultural exhaustion around him, the speaker is understandably dumbstruck by the bird's singing:

> At once a voice arose among
>> The bleak twigs overhead
> In a full-hearted evensong
>> Of joy illimited;
> An aged thrush, frail, gaunt, and small,
>> In blast-beruffled plume,
> Had chosen thus to fling his soul
>> Upon the growing gloom.

Hardy takes scrupulous pains to present the event as the converse opposite to all that precedes it in the poem—through imagery ('arose' counters 'leant' and 'outleant'), through diction ('full-hearted' and 'illimited' offset 'shrunken' and 'fervourless'), and through rhythm (the resilient iambic pulse of that first line and surging enjambements that culminate in the intensive prefix 'il-' sustaining the emphasis on the emotional abandon). In other words, the third stanza violates the speaker's assumption of a decorum between setting and action. The bird's singing, as understood by him, is out of place and logically unaccountable, and he is forced to make sense of it *for himself*.[11]

Consequently, the landscape-setting of bitter waste, decrepitude and defunctive sterility; the appalling physical state of the bird; the transcendent quality of the bird's song—all these images coalesce into an objective equivalent for the speaker's mental and emotional state in the final stanza. He explicitly asserts his essence as a human being by affirming his instincts for dignity, solidarity, beauty and wonder:

> So little cause for carolings
>> Of such ecstatic sound
> Was written on terrestrial things
>> Afar or nigh around,

That I could think there trembled through
        His happy good-night air
Some blessed Hope, whereof he knew
        And I was unaware.

The poem records, but without grandiosely proclaiming, the speaker's capacity for conceiving ('I could think') of another's mode of consciousness, a capacity that was unexpectedly discovered. And that capacity is sufficient to vindicate the humanist speaker's existence as a quest for value and coherence. The speaker's very perception of the bird's sound as 'ecstatic' and 'happy' singing, against the desolation and fervourlessness of the indifferent universe, is already the expression of a cosmic achievement. The appropriate attitude is one neither of optimism, arrogance, nor despair, but of a humanist acceptance, with which 'men [might] look at true things, / And unilluded view things, / And count to bear undue things' ('To Sincerity' [G233]). Only because the humanist speaker is content to recognize 'the Worst' is he content to assert, as courageously as he can, the limitations of his humanity as it confronts a vastly powerful cosmic process. He knows that by boldly and reasonably affirming his essential humanity in spite of what is accidental and irrational ('undue') inside and outside himself,

The real might mend the seeming,
Facts better their foredeeming,
And Life its disesteeming.

In 'The Darkling Thrush', the humanist speaker's response is one of quiet courage and assertiveness because he lives in the present, without myths and inherited consolations. The one thing in the entire scene that corresponds to this speaker's moral being is the song of the thrush, an impulse most decidedly not from a vernal wood, but from a dark coppice. Having critically observed the indifferent, meaningless world about him, and conscious of the vulnerability of the thrush, the speaker interprets the singing as the bird's deliberate and solitary affirmation of the precious essence of itself under extreme conditions. In making this interpretation, the speaker enacts what he himself has 'chosen' to do. Even though his own affirmation can itself have no ultimate effect on the conditions of his existence, the very act of affirming himself brings him a form of consolation, while enlarging the reader's sense of what is humanly. Possible. However, not only does he not need the consolation of some absolute truth, but he would reject any notion of it as a denial of his life. Instead, this humanist speaker claims freedom to create value and coherence for himself in a space beyond cosmic and ethical processes. Accordingly, the world he inhabits remains mysterious and a cause for anxiety; but insofar as there is meaning, it is to be discovered personally, here and now, in the midst of despair. If there is a sin against his individual humanity, it is less despair about this life than 'Some blessed Hope' in another. From the delighted assurance he attributes to the bird the speaker distances himself, aware as he is that the source of his own solace lies within his individual humanity.

In Hardy's humanist lyrics, then, solace comes from a speaker's personal affirmation of a relative valuation made in the face of an uncaring, non-moral universe. Taking a stand against the cosmos, mankind asserts his values and intentions, fragile and limiting though they be. Consequently, the 'figure [that] stands in our van with arm uplifted, to knock us back from any pleasant prospect we indulge in as probable'—the Bunyanesque metaphor for inexorable circumstance that Hardy shared with his mother—has to contend with 'the undeniable necessity of seeing life from the inside of the human psyche rather than from the astronomical-biological perspective of nineteenth century science'.[12]

Notes

9. Johnson's clarifying letter in *The Thomas Hardy Journal*. Cf. *CPW* 3: 366 and Maynard 170.

10. E.g., *King Lear* 1.4.200, *Paradise Lost* 3.39, 'Ode to a Nightingale' (line 51), and 'Dover Beach' (line 35). But see Allingham; Bayley; Ramazani, 'Era' 135.

11. On Hardy's assonance here see Lock 129–30.

12. *PN* 6–7; Schwartz 127.

—Brian Green. From *Hardy's Lyrics: Pearls of Pity*. New York: St. Martin's Press (1996): 120–23.

[Peter Widdowson is the author of *Thomas Hardy* (1996); *Literature* (1999); and co-author of *A Practical Reader in Contemporary Literary Theory* (1996). In the following excerpt, Widdowson the status of despair in "The Darkling Thrush" by comparing it to some of Hardy's neglected poems.]

Let us turn, similarly and finally, to 'The Darkling Thrush' (*PPP*), one of—perhaps *the*—most famous of Hardy's poems.

I leant upon a coppice gate
    When Frost was spectre-gray,
And Winter's dregs made desolate
    The weakening eye of day.
The tangled bine-stems scored the sky
    Like strings of broken lyres,
And all mankind that haunted nigh
    Had sought their household fires.

The land's sharp features seemed to be
    The Century's corpse outleant,
His crypt the cloudy canopy,
    The wind his death-lament.
The ancient pulse of germ and birth
    Was shrunken hard and dry,
And every spirit upon earth
    Seemed fervourless as I.

At once a voice arose among
    The bleak twigs overhead
In a full-hearted evensong
    Of joy illimited;
An aged thrush, frail, gaunt, and small,
    In blast-beruffled plume,
Had chosen thus to fling his soul
    Upon the growing gloom.

So little cause for carolings
    Of such ecstatic sound

Was written on terrestrial things
      Afar or nigh around,
That I could think there trembled through
      His happy good-night air
Some blessed Hope, whereof he knew
      And I was unaware.

                    31 December 1900

In general structure, and certainly in theme, the extensively neglected 'Christmastide' (*WW*)[55] compares closely.

The rain-shafts splintered on me
      As despondently I strode;
The twilight gloomed upon me
      And bleared the blank high-road.
Each bush gave forth, when blown on
      By gusts in shower and shower,
A sigh, as it were sown on
      In handfuls by a sower.

A cheerful voice called, nigh me,
      'A merry Christmas, friend!'—
There rose a figure by me,
      Walking with townward trend,
A sodden tramp's, who, breaking
      Into thin song, bore straight
Ahead, direction taking
      Toward the Casuals' gate.

The first stanza contains as precise and chilling a natural landscape as that in the opening of 'The Darkling Thrush'—although it does not anthropomorphize it in the way the latter does, nor does it give it the symbolic resonance achieved by the somewhat forced phrase 'The Century's corpse outleant'. The famous 'frail, gaunt' thrush's 'carolings' are successfully paralleled by the 'sodden tramp's' 'thin song'—surely an image as, if not more, telling of irrepressible hope as the 'full-hearted evensong' of the thrush. In 'Christmastide' Hardy does not extrapolate a moral as he does in the last four lines of the other poem, leaving it implicit in the (to modern readers, now obscure?) irony of the tramp entering 'the Casuals' gate' of the Workhouse. Perhaps this final obscurity is the reason for the disregard given to a finely understated vignette in contrast to the great fame of the designedly 'public' poem. But perhaps, also, the conventionally received 'Hardy' needs 'Nature' (a thrush) rather than a member of the human underclass (a tramp) to point up the egocentricity of an abstract pessimism? But if it is indeed 'Nature' and philosophical extrapolation that is required, another largely neglected poem, 'The Last Chrysanthemum'—which immediately precedes 'The Darkling Thrush' in *PPP*—supplies both. The description of the flower in the first four stanzas seems to me equal to anything else Hardy wrote in this mode, and the irony of the fifth stanza is handled with the spare lyrical economy so often elsewhere admired in his poetry. But if it is the idiosyncratically obscure final two lines of the poem—'Yet it is but one mask of many worn / By the Great Face behind'—which commit it as a whole to outer darkness, how come we cope elsewhere with 'Doomsters', 'Immanent Will', 'Vast Imbecilities', and so forth (or even with 'The Century's corpse outleant')? Again, as an exercise in explicitly rationalizing our critical discrimination, we should try evaluating the two poems—unranked, unknown, unseen-and then explain their unequal status in Hardy's *oeuvre*.

Finally in the context of 'The Darkling Thrush's apparent preeminence, let me compare with it the once more generally ignored 'On Stinsford Hill at Midnight'.[56]

> I glimpsed a woman's muslined form
>   Sing-songing airily
> Against the moon; and still she sang,
>   And took no heed of me.
>
> Another trice, and I beheld
>   What first I had not scanned,
> That now and then she tapped and shook
>   A timbrel in her hand.
>
> So late the hour, so white her drape,
>   So strange the look it lent

To that blank hill, I could not guess
     What phantastry it meant.

Then burst I forth: 'Why such from you?
     Are you so happy now?'
Her voice swam on; nor did she show
     Thought of me anyhow.

I called again: 'Come nearer; much
     That kind of note I need!'
The song kept softening, loudening on,
     In placid calm unheed.

'What home is yours now?' then I said;
     'You seem to have no care.'
But the wild wavering tune went forth
     As if I had not been there.

'This world is dark, and where you are,'
     I said, 'I cannot be!'
But still the happy one sang on,
     And had no heed of me.

Rhythmically not dissimilar to 'The Darkling Thrush', this mysterious poem makes an almost identical statement to it: the 'heedless' happiness of the song of the thrush/woman suggesting some 'blessed Hope' in this 'dark world' which the 'I' of the poem cannot share. Both poems, it should be noted, remain ambiguous—neither clarifies whether it endorses hope or despondency as the proven reality. While 'On Stinsford Hill' clearly does not have the evocative natural description of the opening stanzas of 'The Darkling Thrush'—which certainly may devalue it for inclusion in the 'characteristic' Hardy—it does, nevertheless, have the mystery of its 'event' lyrically defined by the first three eerie stanzas, redolent as they are of Hardy's much-praised expropriations from the ballad tradition. Two factors suggest themselves as to why, once more, we may find ourselves puzzled and unconvinced by the consensual elevation of one poem and the relegation of the other: *On what grounds?* must be the insistent question. First, Hardy's explanatory subscript note to

'The Darkling Thrush' gives that poem much of its reverberating resonance. Without it, 'The Century's corpse outleant' would be even more obscure than it already is, and the whole poem could be read only speculatively and with great difficulty as a meditation on the turn of the 19th century. Secondly, I would repeat that the 'characteristic'—i.e. 'great'—Hardy seems to need the presence of a voice from 'Nature' (the thrush), and not from a human being (however ghostly). In effect, the 'heedless' happiness of Nature, in its entire alterity from the human, cannot threaten or challenge the validity of the pessimism of the human mind: it is, simply and ironically, *other*. This, then, legitimizes the continued acceptance of despair as a reasonable—perhaps even exemplary—intellectual posture. If, on the other hand, the agent of an alternative 'happiness' or 'hopefulness' is human, then that absolute otherness breaks down, pessimism becomes only one intellectual option amongst others, and can be challenged for its selfishness and passivity. In other words, it can be shown to be able to be vanquished and transcended by the opposite human capacity: that which embraces happiness, hope, futurity, self-determination— everything, in short, that an ideology of quietistic cultural despair rejects. The canonic Hardy, I am arguing by way of 'The Darkling Thrush', tends to underwrite this critical and ideological stance (see Donald Davie above, amongst others rather less self-aware and explicit), while the neglected poems, at least marginally, problematize it.

NOTES

55. Only reprinted in Hynes (ed.) (1984b).
56. Only reprinted in Hynes (ed.) (1984b).

—Peter Widdowson. *Thomas Hardy: Late Essays and Earlier*. New York: St. Martin's Press (1998): 163–67.

BARBARA HARDY ON "THE DARKLING THRUSH" AS A THRESHOLD POEM

[Barbara Hardy is the author of *Tellers and Listeners: The Narrative Imagination* (1975); *Forms of Feeling in Victorian*

Fiction (1985) and *A Reading of Jane Austen* (1979). In the following excerpt from her book, Hardy discusses "The Darkling Thrush" as a threshold poem wherein the poet "hangs on to things as they are."]

The firm line of limit plays a more ambitious part in 'The Darkling Thrush', Hardy's most imaginative bird lyric, already discussed as a reflexive poem. It is also a poem about sympathetic nature which almost but not quite reaches beyond rational limit. The aged gauntness of the thrush and his brave unseasonal song are used expressively to convey wintriness and energy, elderly gloom and a kind of hope. The poem begins with an exaggeratedly wintry setting in which everything is reduced, grey frost, bare stems, day's eye weakened, human beings both absent and ghostlike, has a second stanza in which the century's corpse is a central image, and a last stanza in which the thrush starts up in 'full-hearted evensong / Of joy illimited', only then brought into accord with the scene's austerity, by being aged, frail, gaunt, small and 'In blast-beruffled plume'. He belongs and does not belong to the dreary scene:

> So little cause for carolings
>   Of such ecstatic sound
> Was written on terrestrial things
>   Afar or nigh around,
> That I could think there trembled through
>   His happy goodnight air
> Some blessed Hope, whereof he knew
>   And I was unaware.

It is with the greatest tentativeness that Hardy makes as if to move over the threshold dividing human from other nature, but it is only a gesture of crossing, and he hangs on to things as they are. The thrush's scrawniness is particularized, asserting a physical presence which gives good cover for symbolism, but appearances are preserved, the threshold is not crossed, animal privacy is not penetrated. The human imagination is trying its best—if best is the word—to press against limits of perception and invoke sympathetic nature but Hardy's appreciative and scrupulous recognition of the bird's separateness and difference, stays on the agnostic side of nature's division.

The poet keeps the categories intact and articulates only the possibility of taking the bird as a symbol of optimism. 'Some blessed Hope' is capitalized, and imagined lovingly, but its pressure of wish-fufilment is made clear. This is longing, candidly vague, needy, and tentative. Hope's blessed presence is permitted by the reservation, 'I could think', by the assertion that the creature's affective life—Earth's secret—must stay a mystery. So must the future and the metaphysical meanings. The poem suggests the imaginative limits of that meliorism which Hardy like George Eliot declared to be his stance, and which recognizes speculative limits. The tremor of anthropomorphism reinforces the tremulous cosmic hope but, keeps it in its place. The poem imagines a pressure—the very teleological and Christian pressure Hardy resisted—to be too humanly imaginative about birds' song, so traditionally tempting to poets. If we hear a subdued dialogue with the 'Ode to the Nightingale' ('Darkling, I listen' and 'full-throated ease' behind 'full-hearted joy') it is to remember how that romantic flight touches earth to question its own symbolism, interrogating limit and threshold in ways Hardy would have found congenially scrupulous, 'Fled is that music ... Do I wake or sleep?'

—Barbara Hardy. *Thomas Hardy Imagining Imagination: Hardy's Poetry and Fiction*. London and New Brunswick, NJ: The Athlone Press (2000): 199–200.

JOHN HUGHES ON HARDY'S AMBIVALENT ATTITUDE TOWARDS MUSIC

[John Hughes is the author of *Lines of Flight: Reading Deleuze with Hardy, Gissing, Conrad, and Woolf* (1997). In the following excerpt, Hughes discusses Hardy's ambivalent attitude towards music in "The Darkling Thrush."]

John Bayley's discussion of 'The Darkling Thrush' in *An Essay on Hardy* identifies an inimitable principle of disunity at work in the poem, which he takes as a key to Hardy's characteristic effects in both the poetry and the prose. Bayley writes:

> Throughout his work, the ways in which we are absorbed into it, moved, delighted, are never co-ordinated, never really unified.[1]

Bayley's sustained reading of the poem locates unconsciously produced separations of metaphor and description as the means by which the poem is held between the world of human meanings and consolations, and the bleakly inhospitable winter scene:

> The thrush's song is the climax of this whole tendency; and the thrush himself, in his shrivelled and unkempt physical presence, its leading man. The metaphors are now of religion, of joys and consolations; and we recognise that the poem itself, like not a few of Hardy's, has come to suggest the progression and cadence of a hymn. But the blessed hope appropriate to a hymn is in complete obliviousness of such a song as the bird is singing—its 'happy goodnight air'—a line whose unexpectedness, among the comparatively formal sobriety of the poem's diction, always brings the tears to my eyes. (*An Essay on Hardy*, p. 38)

For Bayley, the 'joy illimited' and hope of the bird's singing are all the More moving for their incongruity and unexpectedness. At this moment, the listener's response is divided between an unillusioned consciousness of things, and a reawakened sense of joy and communion that is oblivious to this. The bird's song signals possibilities that the tentative conclusion of the poem seems concerned to remark, and incorporate, even as it suggests at the same time that such possibilities are unactualisable:

> [...] I could think there trembled through
> > His happy good-night air
> Some blessed Hope, whereof he knew
> > And I was unaware.[2]

So Bayley's discussion is informed by the ideas that the bird's song involves an absent-mindedness at odds with the scene around, and that it transmits a sense of happiness that is both real and insistent, as well as unsustainable within this surrounding physical environment at the end of the century. The song provokes a response, a surprise by joy that the speaker in the poem, fervourless and leaning upon the coppice gate, is painfully aware that he is unable to live up to and translate into a lived experience.

This discussion anticipates important features of the argument which follows, above all that the uses of music in Hardy's work are in many aspects marked by an ambivalent attitude such as Bayley suggests. Music is seen to evoke a response to life that is inseparable from what gives life value, as well as incompatible with Hardy's vision of personal and historical circumstances. Within the sardonic, parodic and ironic operations of the fiction, for instance, and the gaps between memory and actuality in the poetry, music works to evoke necessary potentials of individuality and community. It awakens hopes that are set in a kind of counterpoint to the deadening types of disappointment to which they are subject in what the plots of the fiction, and the scenarios of the poems, ultimately confirm as reality. (…)

The study of music in these texts provides a way of seeing how they open and close between different and disjoined dimensions of time and experience, and allows for an access into what are seen as the fundamental, even constitutive, affective dimensions and concerns of Hardy's writing. As this suggests, this book presents itself less as a study of the representation of music in Hardy's fiction and poetry simply, than as one that explores the connection between music and emotion within his work.[3] The aim thereby is to approach Hardy's abiding concern with individual expression, and his recurrent themes—time, community, and love—through this connection.

With respect to these affective features in Hardy's work, for instance, it is doubtful that there is any poem of Hardy's, even the most explicitly grief-stricken, which, for all its conscious sense of loss, does not secrete within itself coexisting, and primarily unconscious, elements of joy or ecstasy. Another remark of Bayley's, along the lines that disappointment is a characteristic effect of form in Hardy, suggests Hardy's often unsparing treatment of human aspirations.[4] At the same time, though, it suggests the opposite, the extent to which Hardy's texts depend on pursuing fugitive effects of pleasure, and presentiments of happiness. Hardy the poet, like his fictional characters and his readers, is constantly overtaken by this elating sense of the possible, by moments of enthusiasm that imply a distinctive conception and evaluation of life. Given the broad range of ways in which music's 'insistent calls of joy' function in Hardy's work (*Complete Poems*, p. 876), this Introduction offers itself as a kind of overture, indicating some of the main questions and motifs which are developed in the book as a whole. (…)

Thus, to examine the elements of joy in 'The Darkling Thrush' is not to deny the prevailingly sombre mood of the scene in the poem, nor the dominant tenor of its conclusions and imagery. Indeed, because of these features Peter Widdowson has pointed out that it is a poem which has been deployed as a kind of model case, by those with an interest in the ideologically limiting construction of Hardy as a pessimist. The poem is taken as one which 'legitimizes the continued acceptance of despair as a reasonable—perhaps even exemplary—intellectual position'.[6] On this reading, skepticism, and age cannot attain to any 'blessed Hope', and the only lyres in the poem are the broken ones made up by the tangled bine-stems. Nonetheless, as Widdowson also emphasizes, Hardy's poetry in general can be seen as shot through with the 'opposite […] capacity: to embrace happiness, hope, futurity, self-determination'. My concern here is to stress how this opposite strain manifests itself even in 'The Darkling Thrush' in various ways, contributing to the circulation between incommensurable attitudes and moments of experience that defines Hardy's poetic vision. While there is in the scene nothing to endorse the inconvenient and inconsequential promptings of joy that arise from the bird's 'carolings', the interesting fact is that the poem appears equally to encompass the contrary truth that these promptings are irresistible. They can be neither dismissed nor finally comprehended. Accordingly, the song of the bird sets up an oscillation, between the inspired and the grimly literal, that is evident in many and minute ways in the poem, as in the four lines below. There, the intricate felicities of sound and suggestion of the first two lines yield, in the last pair, to a more down to earth appraisal, a returning sense of the separated and drained elements of the scene:

> So little cause for carolings
>> Of such ecstatic sound
> Was written on terrestrial things
>> Afar or nigh around [...]

Further, it is certainly true that in hundreds of poems, and in nearly all the fiction, music provides a kind of *topos* for the scenes and plots which play out, arrange, these discordances of different qualities of feeling and of thought. Music recurrently, if temporarily, brings about an enhanced sense of individuality and affinity.

Notes

1. John Bayley, *An Essay on Hardy* (Cambridge: Cambridge University Press, 1978), p. 40.

2. Thomas Hardy, *The Complete Poems* (edited by James Gibson, London: Macmillan, 1976), p. 150.

3. So there will be many points in the discussions which follow where I acknowledge the influential work of the many critics (Grundy, Pinion, Gatrell, Shelman, Mitchell, and Jackson-Houlston among them) who have offered this direct kind of engagement with music in Hardy's work.

4. Bayley distinguishes Hardy from writers such as Powys, Lawrence and Faulkner for whose readers:

> [d]isappointment, if it comes, is thus a complete thing: a boredom with, or alienation from, the text. In Hardy, disappointment is a reaction much more intimate and intermingled, which may turn out to present itself as an actual asset, a greater clarity in the experience of the pleasure. (*An Essay on Hardy*, p. 4)

6. Thomas Hardy, *Selected Poetry and Non-Fictional Prose* (edited by Peter Widdowson, London: Macmillan, 1997), p. 215.

> —John Hughes. *'Ecstatic Sound': Music and Individuality in the Work of Thomas Hardy.* Burlington, Vermont: Ashgate Publishing Company (2001): 1–4.

CRITICAL ANALYSIS OF

"Afterwards"

"Afterwards," the closing poem in the volume *Moments of Vision*, was sent to the publisher in the summer of 1917, when Hardy was seventy-seven years old. It is patterned on the pastoral elegy, a genre of poetry dating back to classical times, but with many ironic transformations. Perhaps the most striking feature of "Afterwards" is that the one being eulogized is the poet himself, speculating on what his death will mean to others and if he will be remembered. The main premise of this poem works through the rhetorical device known as prolepsis, a figure of thought in which future events are expressed as if they had already taken place.

The conventional pastoral elegy is a ceremonial mourning of an exemplary figure, in this instance the poet himself. Its basic features include a procession of mourners, appeals and questionings of witnesses, outbreaks of anger or emotion, expressions of tribute and the use of natural imagery in a world which can be seen as the site of renewal or loss. For all its gentleness in tone, the simple country setting is not as ideal as it first appears, for these docile creatures are endangered and there is, indeed, strife in this otherwise bucolic setting. "He strove that such innocent creatures should / come to no harm." And that same precarious situation may become more so after the speaker's death, as he presents himself as the protector of the gentle creatures. "Afterwards" is very much concerned with the plight of animals and the hope that others will continue to care for their welfare. In fact, in 1923, Thomas Hardy was asked to become a vice-president of the Animal Defence and Anti-Vivisection League. Wanting to maintain a moderate position on an impassioned issue, Hardy's response was a conditional acceptance, in which he expressed a wish to approve experimentation only for those instances which involved a minimum of suffering and only where the goal would be a benefit to both men and animal. "There could be nothing more reasonable, and it should be noted that Tom did not ask that any more violence be directed against animals than a human being might be asked to endure. Like many others ... he was horrified by the ill-treatment accorded to horses in war, and wrote of it often, particularly to Florence Henniker" (Seymour-Smith).

The first stanza is Hardy's imaginative rendering of his final departure from the world in springtime. It could more appropriately be seen as his leave-taking rather than his death, cast within a pastoral setting. Interestingly, as the very first line indicates, the poet has already departed, gently through a gate distinct from the main entrance, and personifies "the Present" as the one left behind. "When the Present has latched its postern behind my tremulous stay." Furthermore, though tremulous describes an aged poet, it also hints at a wish that others will be susceptible to his influence in his love and devotion to Nature. "And the May month flaps its glad green leaves like wings, / ... will the neighbors say, 'He was a man who used to notice such things'?" The simile is unexpected and embellished by alliteration.

As the poet is uncertain of the time in year in which he will pass on, the second stanza begins the first of three other scenarios in conformity with the season and posits the first of three conditional statements that begin with "if." Following the springtime setting of the previous stanza, Hardy turns his attention to the sights and sounds of a summer evening and again envisions his death as a leave-taking, quiet and unobtrusive. "If it be in the dusk when, like an eyelid's soundless blink, / [when] the dewfall-hawk comes crossing the shades." And, as he will do in each subsequent stanza, Hardy expresses a wish that a solitary observer will remember his devotion to these innocent creatures and think "'[t]o him thus must have been a familiar sight.'"

The third stanza envisions the poet's death as taking place in autumn and evokes the gentleness of a "nocturnal blackness, mothy and warm, / When the hedgehog travels furtively over the lawn." However, an interesting pattern begins to emerge as we observe the familiar wish to be remembered for all that he has done to protect "such innocent creatures" as being susceptible to a diminution in each succeeding stanza. The man who used to actively notice such things in the beginning of the poem is only assumed to have been familiar with the sights and sounds of nature in the second stanza and, in this third stanza, is said to have accomplished very little though he had the best of intentions. "'He strove that such innocent creatures should / come to no harm, / But he could do little for them; and now he is gone.'" Hardy's use of the word "strove" has particular significance within a pastoral context where animals are safe and cared for. The notion of the poet striving on behalf of the animals disrupts the serene pastoral setting, bringing violence, conflict, and spiritual struggle into a supposedly placid environment. There is strife in Hardy's countryside, a world with no guarantees.

The fourth stanza envisions the poet's death against the background of a winter landscape. His imagined departure takes place during the time of "the full-starred heavens that winter sees," while the neighbors, who have merely heard of his passing, remain outside his door. The increasing passivity on the part of others, who should remember his devotion to Nature, is expressed through the poet's doubts that they will continue the good work he leaves behind. "Will this thought rise on those who will meet my face no more, 'He was one who had an eye for such mysteries.'?" By now, the poet is highly doubtful that his friends and acquaintances will remember at all what he strove to accomplish, as is evidenced by the question mark following the poem's familiar refrain.

In the fifth and final stanza, the poet's earthly existence has already ended. His announcement of his own death is expressed euphemistically, in gentle pastoral terms. The "bell of quittance" having already been rung, Hardy envisions his release from all mortal cares and concerns. He is now free to return a part of nature, a spirit that attempts to make its presence known while hovering over his former domicile, "a crossing breeze [which] cuts a pause in its outrollings," but has no confidence that they will recognize his return as a spiritual presence while they remain in their earthly existence. "And will any say ... / Till they rise again, as they were a new bell's boom, / 'He hears it not now, but used to notice such things?'"

CRITICAL VIEWS ON
"Afterwards"

MERRYN WILLIAMS ON CURIOUS OPTIMISM

[Merryn Williams is the author of *Thomas Hardy and Rural England* (1972); *Women in the English Novel, 1800–1900* (1984); and *Margaret Oliphant: A Critical Biography* (1986). In the following excerpt, Williams discusses the curious optimism of "Afterwards."]

Afterwards

DATE   First published in 1917. Hardy was in his mid-seventies when he wrote 'Afterwards' and in some ways it is a deliberate valediction. In the nature of things, he felt, it was not very likely that he had much more time ahead (though he did, in fact, live for another ten years).

STYLE   The movement of this poem is slow, gentle, and rather hesitating (perhaps Hardy's own word, 'tremulous', is the best one to use). The images in each verse are the most memorable part of it, and these build up an impression that Hardy is, not exactly confident, but at least hopeful that he will be remembered by a few people, not as a poet or novelist but simply as a loving. Observer of nature.

SUBJECT   In its quiet way, this is a curiously optimistic poem, and one which is concerned not so much with death as with the possibilities of life. Each verse gives a different picture of the world he will be leaving, and these pictures are very moving and convincing. The real focus of interest is not himself, but the animals, birds, leaves and stars.

There is a distinct feeling of gaiety in the first verse, that we might not expect in a poem which is 'about' death. 'The May month flaps its glad green leaves like wings,'—Hardy sees this happening after he is gone, just as the bells of Christminster rang 'joyously' when Jude was in his coffin, and does not resent it at all. He only hopes that it may bring him to mind momentarily, because he was 'a man who use to notice such things'. In the rest of the poem there is more evidence that he was, in fact, a keen observer of the world around him. For example, how many of us would think of comparing the flight of a hawk to an *eyelid*? But this image very skillfully evokes the ideas of speed and soundlessness.

Hardy was fond of hedgehogs, and throughout his life campaigned vigorously against cruelty to animals and birds. Many people were amused when, asked for his comments on modern warfare, he suggested that armies should at least stop using horses on the battlefield. In the third verse of 'Afterwards', he recognizes that he could do little for dumb animals, but, at the same time, holds on to his belief that even a hedgehog has a right to live, and a value and worth of its own.

The fourth verse moves out from the homely image of hedgehogs and moths on the lawn of Hardy's house to the 'mystery' of the starry sky, and the questions it raises in our minds about man's place in the universe, which he had described, long before, in *Far from the Madding Crowd* (though it is characteristic that, in the last verse of all, he should move back from this to the familiar sound of bells from a country church). It is not a religious image; after all those years of searching, Hardy felt that he was still no nearer an answer to 'the eternal question of what Life was, and why we were there'. He can only comment on the everyday things which he does understand, and keep his sense of wonder in the face of the unknown. The poem makes no dogmatic statements. It merely suggests, rather tentatively, that an individual man can make only the faintest of marks on the universe, and that the most he can hope for is to be remembered with kindness by a few people after he dies. It also suggests that there is nothing tragic about this; if anything, it is a happy thing, when the time comes, to be absorbed back into the natural world.

This is what happens to most of us, of course, but it has not in fact happened to Hardy. One of the most modest of men, he would not have thought of claiming, like Shakespeare, 'Not marble nor the gilded monuments / Of princes shall outlive this powerful rhyme', even though in his case it was true. 'Afterwards' is among the small group of Hardy poems which make his place in literature secure.

—Merryn Williams. *A Preface to Hardy*. Essex, UK: Pearson Education Limited (1993): 167–69.

TREVOR JOHNSON ON HARDY'S FAMILY HISTORY

[Trevor Johnson is the author of *Thomas Hardy* (1968) and *Joseph Andrews by Henry Fielding (A Critical Guide)* (1987). In the following excerpt from his book, Johnson discusses "Afterwards" as a poem about Hardy's family history.]

AUTOBIOGRAPHICAL POEMS

Speaking generally there is more autobiography in a hundred lines of the poetry than in all the novels.

Life, p. 392

In the broad sense Havelock Ellis used when he wrote of Tolstoy 'Every artist is his own biographer', Hardy's remark is doubtless true. Setting aside the manifestly fictitious narratives, anecdotes and ballads, virtually all of Hardy's poems tell us *something* of his intellectual, spiritual or emotional pilgrimage through life. But a narrower definition of autobiography is needed to make this section manageable and, since the love poetry has a chapter to itself, I shall begin with that small, but highly significant, group of poems which treat directly of what might be called Hardy's family history. Not that they are simply word-portraits: all include Hardy's comments or reflections. But family memories and associations were a kind of piety to Hardy who once wrote 'Clouds, mist and mountains are unimportant besides the wear on a threshold or the print of a hand, and a beloved relative's old battered tankard is entirely superior to the finest Greek vase.' By 'superior' he did not, of course, mean 'more beautiful', but possessing an evocative power stemming from what he once called 'memorial associations'. So, to recall and record his kin and what passed between him and them, often long since, was to establish the only lien on immortality that they, and he, could hope for. Fascinated, as his poem of that title attests, by heredity, a sedulous genealogist, he added to these interests something approaching total recall, a strong 'attachment to the soil of one particular spot', and an affection as deep-rooted as it was clear-sighted. Often these qualities of mind conspire to produce glimpses of people, 'in their habits as they lived', drawn up from the distant past with an uncanny immediacy which we have already encountered in Chapter 2 with *The Self-Unseeing* (135).

This imaginative acuity of vision which compels us to see as he does, is one of Hardy's greatest assets as a writer; by virtue of it his prose also often verges on and occasionally becomes, poetry. Yet with it goes an unusual objectivity. Hardy very rarely enlists our sympathy, still less our admiration, for himself. Yet though he contemplates his former self quite disinterestedly, his attitude is far from detached in the sense of cold or hard; warmth, tolerance, muted humour, and a love not the less profound for being inexplicit, all come together in these retrospective encounters. For, as he confesses in *The Ghost of the Past* (249fW/H/*), 'We two kept house, the Past and I, // There was in that, companionship // Something of ecstasy.' (…)

Afterwards (511/ALL/H/*)

Because Hardy's emendations here are so crucial I print all the important ones below, listing line numbers and giving the final text in italics too, where necessary.

Line 1 MS reads 'when night has closed its shutters on my dismantled day'.

Line 3 MS reads 'people' (*for neighbours*).

Line 7 MS reads 'nibbled' (*for wind-warped*).

Line 17 MS reads 'passing bell' (*for bell of quittance*).

Line 18 MS reads 'makes a break in its utterings' (*for cuts a pause, outrollings*).

Hardy's epitaph on himself, it was written in his seventy-seventh year. But it is not the author and public figure on the aftermath of whose death he speculates; these are far from the expectations of a vain or ambitious man hungry for posthumous fame. Indeed the poem is nearer the verbal equivalent of a shrug; death itself is dismissed offhandedly. Moreover, even though *He was a man who used to notice such things* is, in all conscience, a profoundly modest assessment, Hardy could not be certain even of so much. He leaves the posthumous judgement to those country/*neighbours* (a deliberate choice, as the MS line 3 shows us) for whom Hardy was a local lad who had done well out of writing books. He hopes they may recall his keenness of eye, his care for small creatures as they might a shepherd's or a ploughman's.

This approach requires him to efface himself from the poem in so far as overt emotion is concerned. He creates a detached mood also by his employment of an exceptionally slow-paced, almost ambling, line, which invests the whole poem with a musing, speculative tone, sprinkled as it is with *If, may*, and *will?* He 'asserts nothing'; in one of his own phrases this is a 'last look round' familiar, loved terrain, which perhaps no one, before or since, has known better.

Such a survey was bound to include much natural imagery, and he never bettered his impressions of the May month in the first verse, where *delicate-filmed* and *new-spun* display his genius for the compound epithet, subsequently seen in *wind-warped* and *full-starred* (if perhaps a trifle less effective in *dew-fall hawk*, where *hawk* does not, to my mind, primarily suggest a moth.) Nevertheless, meticulously as he depicts the minutiae of the scene, this is very much more than 'nature poetry'. After the first verse the prevailing atmosphere becomes that of dusk or night. All is blurred and hushed; to use his own words, *nocturnal* and *tremulous*, no doubt because he wishes to impart a sense of the mysterious, fleeting nature of life itself. The language he uses to enhance this mood is at times miraculous. To apostrophise night as *mothy and warm*, to compare a moth's almost imperceptible arrival to an *eyelid's soundless blink*, is to add a dimension to our own imperfect perception of the physical world. It is in this way that a man who was shy and tentative in his personal relationships allows us an oblique insight into the mind of a poet who was, in Coventry Patmore's phrase, one 'singularly moved // To love the lovely that is not beloved.'

Hardy's emendations bear out what I have said. In the first, and therefore very important, line, Hardy initially failed to create quite the right sinuous flow—the metre is a very delicate and subtle one. But though the revision is smoother to the ear, he may also have felt *Night* (as an 'elegant variation' on death) was a near-cliché. Attempting to invigorate it by the metaphors of *closed its shutters* and *dismantled* he found himself arousing undertones of shops and machinery. To substitute *the Present* (for *Night*) was neat and a gain in precision (the Present *releases* us, Night *receives* us) but the revised line as a whole is masterly. For a *postern* was a small, subsidiary exit for unimportant guests, *latched* implies a casual dismissal, and *tremulous stay*, with its undertones of insecurity, impermanence, physical frailty and fear, imparts exactly that universal feeling which the Bible sums up in the famous verse, 'I am a stranger here and a sojourner, as all my fathers were.' 'Nibbled' (i.e. by sheep) was good, but *wind-warped* (hinting at an identification of the *thorn* with Hardy) is better, while his invention of *bell of quittance* adds the suggestion of debts cancelled to the ancient custom of the *passing bell*. Finally, *cuts a break* avoids the implicit contradiction in *makes a blank* (can you *make* something nonexistent?), and where *utterings* would humanise it, *outrollings* perfectly captures the sound of the *bell's boom*.

The abiding impression is one of quiet truthfulness, a particularly rare achievement in a poem as directly personal as this in its subject. As C. Day Lewis wisely said, this genre is especially perilous to poets because, in it 'false humility, egotism or emotional insincerity cannot be hidden.'

—Trevor Johnson. *A Critical Introduction to the Poems of Thomas Hardy.* New York: St. Martin's Press, Inc. (1991): 55–56 and 72–4.

[Barbara Hardy is the author of *Tellers and Listeners: The Narrative Imagination* (1975); *Forms of Feeling in Victorian Fiction* (1985) and *A Reading of Jane Austen* (1979). In the following excerpt from her book, Hardy discusses "Afterwards" as Hardy's modest self-elegy.]

Hardy liked to imagine his own ghost, crossing the barrier between life and death. He usually does so playfully, though his play is often wry, and he most strikingly imagines life after his death not as survival but as other people's memory. For example, the elegiac imagination has seldom been imaged with more tact and reserve than in 'Afterwards'. It is a self-elegy, as modest as possible, and involves taking a step beyond the present self:

> When the Present has latched its postern behind my tremulous
> stay,
> And the May month flaps its glad green leaves like wings,
> Delicate-filmed as new-spun silk, will the neighbours say,
> 'He was a man who used to notice such things'?

That image of the gate is like everything in the poem, gentle and soft, the postern latched as if going were as tremulous as staying. 'Tremulous' is a word which works hard, conveying both the beats of being, as Hardy phrased it in 'The Dead Man Walking', and their fragile brevity. The controlled sibilants and the metaphor of latching create an unobtrusive and modest exit, leaving the scene without fuss or disturbance while generously welcoming the cheerful May whose young leaves are appropriately delicate and fragile. Hardy writes about life and about leaving life, bestowing the utmost tenderness on the natural world while also suggesting solicitude for his own modestly imagined memorial. (He is not always modest about this: in 'A Poet' he speaks of a dead poet beloved by 'two bright-souled women', but 'Afterwards' is a far cry from this naïve sultanlike proposal.) Its speaker is treating a difficult subject, however, as he speculates on the touchy subject of personal posthumous praise. One of his solutions is to leave out the expected obituary. This anticipation of becoming a memory is marked by the conspicuous absence of any mention of what Thomas Hardy was and is remembered for—his writing.

The poet leaves out his poetry. The teller leaves out his tales. But in doing he creates an absence which is noticeable, which draws attention to itself, and so is filled. As we read the poem we are likely to notice what it did not anticipate us remembering him for—and here the 'us' stands both for those who knew and those who did not know him. We are also likely to look for traces of the expected desire, and to contemplate those modest natural images afresh, absence desiring and becoming presence in a delicate sly transformation. The images of the poem belong to a perception of the natural world, but may also take Hardy's reader back to his poetry and novels:

> If it be in the dusk when, like an eyelid's soundless blink,
>> The dewfall-hawk comes crossing the shades to alight
> Upon the wind-warped upland thorn, a gazer may think,
>> 'To him this must have been a familiar sight'.

> If I pass during some nocturnal blackness, mothy and warm,
>> When the hedgehog travels furtively over the lawn,
>>> One may say, 'He strove that such innocent creatures
>>> should come to no harm,
>> But he could do nothing for them; and now he is gone'.

> If, when hearing that I have been stilled at last,
>> they stand at the door,
>> Watching the full-starred heavens that winter sees,
> Will this thought rise on those who will meet my face no more,
>> 'He was one who had an eye for such mysteries'?

> And will any say when my bell of quittance is heard in the gloom,
>> And a crossing breeze cuts a pause in its outrollings,
> Till they swell again, as they were a new bell's boom,
>> 'He hears it not now, but used to notice such things'?

The new leaves, the flying hawk, the small mammal, stars, skies and bells are all images active in his writing, though belonging to many observant country dwellers' experience. The imagined moderate praise comes from acquaintances and neighbours, but can fit the experience of strangers and readers too: 'He was a man who used to ...', 'To him this must have been'.... 'He strove ... could do but little'. The 'eye for such mysteries' is a testimony to his yearnings and recognitions of limits, too. Of course it is not necessary to see these images as artistically reflexive, but once we think of it, they are, recalling such episodes as the wonderful Mayday at the end of *The Return of the Native*, the starry nights when Gabriel Oak watches his flocks, Marty's woodlands, Jude's pity for the birds, and Tess's fellow-feelings for trees and animals, and the sound of many bells. The images modestly generalize and assert typicality, in 'such things', but the old familiar Hardy images are being made new, in the poem. Phenomena are perceived very closely, with soft-fingered gentle delicacy, 'delicate-filmed', 'like an eyelid's soundless blink', 'mothy', and by seasoned observation and routines, 'the dewfall hawk' ... and 'The wind-warped upland thorn', the wonderfully observed breeze cutting 'a pause' in the bell's toll and loving apprehensive sympathy with small creatures, for the hedgehog travelling furtively. Like the mysteries, the specific details are appropriate, and the projected hesitant memorial compounds the good habits of elegiac and funereal recapitulation. Hardy is writing his own elegy, with extraordinary but effective tact and understatement, and also making it psychologically exact, alert and healthy by its wondering and self-cheering tone. The ego's anticipation implies, 'What will they say?' and answers, 'Perhaps it won't be too bad: at least they might say this.' It is significantly much less morbid than many of his poems about staying alive. To meditate an elegy for his own passage summoned up the desires and wrung recognitions of a lifetime, but also gave some relief.

—Barbara Hardy. *Thomas Hardy Imagining Imagination: Hardy's Poetry and Fiction.* London and New Brunswick, NJ: The Athlone Press (2000): 188–91.

WORKS BY

Thomas Hardy

The Poor Man and the Lady, 1867 (never published).

Desperate Remedies, 1871 (published anonymously).

Far From the Madding Crowd, 1874.

The Return of the Native, 1878.

The Trumpet-Major, 1880.

A Laodicean, 1881.

Two on a Tower, 1882.

The Mayor of Casterbridge, 1886.

The Woodlanders, 1887.

Wessex Tales, 1888.

Tess of the d'Urbervilles, 1891.

A Group of Noble Dames, 1891.

Life's Little Ironies, 1894.

Jude the Obscure, 1895.

The Well-Beloved, 1897.

Wessex Poems, 1898.

Poems of the Past and the Present, 1901.

The Dynasts, 1904 (part I).

The Dynasts, 1906 (parts II and III).

Time's Laughingstocks, 1909.

A Changed Man, 1913.

Satires of Circumstance, 1914.

Selected Poems, 1916.

Moments of Vision, 1917.

The Famous Tragedy of the Queen of Cornwall, 1923.

Human Shows, 1925.

Winter Words, 1928.

The Early Life of Thomas Hardy, 1928.

The Later Years of Thomas Hardy, 1930.

WORKS ABOUT

Thomas Hardy

Abercrombie, Lascelles. *Thomas Hardy: A Critical Study*. London: M. Secker, 1912.

Bailey, J.O. *The Poetry of Thomas Hardy: A Handbook and Commentary*. Chapel Hill: University of North Carolina Press, 1970.

Berger, Sheila. *Thomas Hardy and Visual Structures: Framing, Disruption, Process*. New York: New York University Press, 1990.

Blackmur, R.P. "The Shorter Poems of Thomas Hardy." *The Expense of Greatness*. Gloucester, MA: Peter Smith, 1958.

Bowra, C.M. "The Lyrical Poetry of Thomas Hardy." *Inspiration and Poetry*. London: Macmillan; New York: St. Martin's Press, 1955.

Casagrande, Peter J. "Hardy's Wordsworth: A Record and a Commentary." *English Literature in Transition* 20 (1977): 210–37.

Chew, Samuel C. *Thomas Hardy, Poet and Novelist*. New York: Russell & Russell, 1928.

Clark, Susan L. *Thomas Hardy and the Tristan Legend*. Heidelberg: C. Winter, 1983.

Collins, Deborah L. *Thomas Hardy and His God: A Liturgy of Unbelief*. New York: St. Martin's Press, 1990.

Cox, Reginald Gordon, ed. *Thomas Hardy, The Critical Heritage*. London: Routledge & K. Paul; New York: Barnes & Noble, 1970.

Daleski, Hillel Matthew. *Thomas Hardy and Paradoxes of Love*. Columbia: University of Missouri Press, 1997.

Das, Manas Mukul. *Thomas Hardy: Poet of Tragic Vision*. Atlantic Highlands, N.J.: Humanities Press, 1983.

Davie, Donald. *Thomas Hardy and British Poetry*. New York: Oxford University Press, 1972.

————. "Hardy's Virgilian Purples." *Agenda* 10, nos. 2–3 (1972): 138–56.

Draper, Jo. *Thomas Hardy's England*. London: J. Cape, 1984.

Elliott, Ralph Warren Victor. *Thomas Hardy's English*. Oxford, England: B. Blackwell in association with Andre Deutsch, 1984.

Entice, Andrew. *Thomas Hardy, Landscapes of the Mind*. London: MacMillan Press, 1979.

Gibson, James. "*Wessex Poems*, 1898." *The Achievement of Thomas Hardy*. Edited by Phillip Mallet. New York: St. Martin's Press, LLC, 2000.

————. *Thomas Hardy: A Literary Life*. New York: St. Martin's Press, 1996.

————. *The Variorum Edition of the Complete Poems of Thomas Hardy*. New York: Macmillan, 1979.

Gatrell, Simon. *Thomas Hardy and the Proper Study of Mankind*. Charlottesville: University Press of Virginia, 1993.

Gibson, *James. Thomas Hardy: A Literary Life*. New York: St. Martin's Press, 1996.

Gittings, Robert. *Thomas Hardy's Later Years*. Boston: Little Brown, 1978.

Goode, John. *Thomas Hardy: The Offensive Truth*. Oxford and New York: B. Blackwell, 1988.

Guerard, Albert J. "The Illusion of Simplicity: The Poetry of Thomas Hardy." *Thomas Hardy*. Edited by Albert J. Gerard. Englewood Cliffs, N.J.: (1963): 160–89.

Halliday, Frank Ernest. *Thomas Hardy: His Life and Work*. New York: Barnes & Noble, 1972.

Hands, Timothy. *Thomas Hardy: Distracted Preacher?: Hardy's Religious Biography and its Influence on his Novels*. New York: St. Martin's Press, 1989.

Hardy, Barbara Nathan. *Thomas Hardy: Imagining Imagination: Hardy's Poetry and Fiction*. London; New Brunswick, New Jersey: Somerset, New Jersey: Athlone Press: Distributed in the U.S. by Transaction Publishers, 2000.

Hardy, Evelyn. *Thomas Hardy: A Critical Biography*. New York: St. Martin's Press, 1954.

Holland, Clive. *Thomas Hardy, O.M.: The Man, his Works, and the Land of Wessex*. New York: Haskell House, 1966.

Howe, Irving. *Thomas Hardy*. New York: Macmillan, 1967.

Hynes, Samuel. *The Pattern of Hardy's Poetry*. Chapel Hill: University of North Carolina Press, 1961.

———. "The Hardy Tradition in Modern English Poetry." *Thomas Hardy: The Writer and His Background*. New York: St. Martin's Press, 1980.

Jedrzejewski, Jan. *Thomas Hardy and the Church*. New York: St. Martin's Press, 1996.

Johnson, Trevor. *A Critical Introduction to the Poems of Thomas Hardy*. New York: St. Martin's Press, Inc., 1991.

Karlin, Danny. "The Figure of the Singer in the Poetry of Thomas Hardy." *The Achievement of Thomas Hardy*. Edited by Phillip Mallet. New York: St. Martin's Press, LLC (2000): 117–36.

Langbaum, Robert Woodrow. *Thomas Hardy in Our Time*. New York: St. Martin's Press, 1995.

Lefebure, Molly. *Thomas Hardy's World: The Life, Times and Works of the Great Novelist and Poet*. London: Carlton Books, 1997.

Lerner, *Laurence. Thomas Hardy's The Mayor of Casterbridge: Tragedy or Social History?* London: Published for Sussex University Press by Chatto & Windus, 1975.

Maynard, Katherine Kearney. *Thomas Hardy's Tragic Poetry: The Lyrics and "The Dynasts."* Iowa City: University of Iowa Press, 1991.

Milberg-Kaye, Ruth. *Thomas Hardy—Myths of Sexuality*. New York: J. Jay Press, 1983.

Millgate, Michael. *Thomas Hardy: A Biography*. New York: Random House, 1982.

———, ed. *Letters of Emma and Florence Hardy*. New York: Oxford University Press, 1996.

Miller, J. Hillis. *Thomas Hardy: Distance and Desire*. Cambridge,

Massachusetts: Belknap Press of Harvard University Press, 1970.

Morrell, Roy. *Thomas Hardy: The Will and the Way*. Kuala Lumpur, University of Malaya Press: Sole distributors: Oxford University Press: London and NewYork, 1968.

O'Neill, Patricia. "Thomas Hardy: Poetics of a Postromantic." *Victorian Poetry* 27, no. 2 (Summer 1989): 129–45.

O'Sullivan, *Timothy. Thomas Hardy: An Illustrated Biography*. New York: St. Martin's Press, 1976.

Page, Norman, ed. *Thomas Hardy: Family History*. London: Routledge/Thoemmes Press, 1998.

Paul, Tom. *Thomas Hardy, The Poetry of Perception*. Totowa, N.J.: Rowman and Littlefield, 1975.

Pinion, F.B., ed. *Thomas Hardy and the Modern World*. Dorchester: Thomas Hardy Society, 1974.

———. *Thomas Hardy: Art and Thought*. Totowa, New Jersey: Rowman and Littlefield, 1977.

———. *A Thomas Hardy Dictionary With Maps and a Chronology*. New York: New York University Press, 1989.

———. *Thomas Hardy: His Life and Friends*. New York: St. Martin's Press, 1992.

Purdy, Richard *Little. Thomas Hardy: A Bibliographical Study*. London and New York: Oxford University Press, 1954.

Ramazani, Jahan. "Hardy and the Poetics of Melancholia: Poems of 1912–13 and Other Elegies for Emma." *ELH*, 58 (1991): 957–77.

Richardson, James. *Thomas Hardy: The Poetry of Necessity*. Chicago: University of Chicago Press, 1977.

Robinson, Jeremy. *Thomas Hardy and John Cowper Powys: Wessex Revisited*. Kidderminster: Crescent moon, 2nd ed., 1994.

Rutland, *William* R. *Thomas Hardy: A Study of His Writings and Their Background*. New York: Russell & Russell, 1962.

Steward, John Innes Mackintosh. *Thomas Hardy: A Critical Biography*. London: Longman, 1971.

Seymour-Smith, Martin. *Hardy*. London: Bloomsbury Publishing Limited, 1994.

Taylor, Dennis. *Hardy's Poetry, 1860–1928*. London and Basingstoke: Macmillan, 1981.

———. *Hardy's Metres and Victorian Prosody*. Oxford: Clarendon Press, 1988.

White, Reginald James. *Thomas Hardy and History*. New York: Barnes and Noble, 1974.

Williams, Merryn. *Thomas Hardy and Rural England*. New York: Columbia University Press, 1972.

———. *A Preface to Hardy*. Essex, UK: Pearson Education Limited, 1993.

Zietlow, Paul. *Moments of Vision: The Poetry of Thomas Hardy*. Cambridge, MA: Harvard University Press, 1974.

ACKNOWLEDGMENTS

Introduction from *A Map of Misreading* by Harold Bloom: pp. 19–24. © 1975, 2003 by Oxford University Press. Reprinted by permission of the author.

A Journey Into Thomas Hardy's Poetry by Joanna Cullen Brown: pp. 175–178, 194–196, 272–273, 295–297. © 1989 by Joanna Cullen Brown. Reprinted by permission.

Hardy's Literary Language and Victorian Philology by Dennis Taylor: pp. 300–301, 275–277. © 1993 by Dennis Taylor. Published by Oxford University Press 1993. Reprinted by permission.

Thomas Hardy in Our Time by Robert Langbaum: pp. 45, 51–53. © 1995 by Robert Langbaum. Reprinted with permission of Palgrave Macmillan.

Moments of Vision: The Poetry of Thomas Hardy by Paul Zeitlow: pp. 58–61. © 1974 by Harvard University Press. Reprinted by permission.

The Patterns of Hardy's Poetry by Samuel Hynes: pp. 44–49, 123–126, 136–137. © 1956 by the University of North Carolina Press. Used by permission of the publisher.

The Poetry of Thomas Hardy: A Handbook and Commentary by J.O. Bailey: pp. 51–54, 55–56. © 1970 by the University of North Carolina Press. Used by permission of the publisher.

A Critical Introduction to The Poems of Thomas Hardy by Trevor Johnson: pp. 55–56, 72–74, 178–179. © 1991 by Henry Anthony Trevor Johnson. Reprinted with permission of Palgrave Macmillan.

The Romantic Tradition in Modern English Poetry: Rhetoric and Experience by Geoffrey Harvey: pp. 53–55, 66–69. © 1986 by Geoffrey Harvey. Reprinted with permission of Palgrave Macmillan.

"Hardy Ruins: Female Spaces and Male Designs" by U.C. Knoepflmacher. From *PMLA* vol. 105, no. 5, October 1990: pp.

Themes and Ideas